SINGLE
WOMAN
HOMESTEADER

LEONA DIXON COX

Illustrations by David N. Giles

Foreword by Marjorie Gordon

Dobbins, CA 95935

Published by **Inkwell**
P.O. Box 178, Dobbins, CA 95935

Editor: Marjorie Gordon.
Picture editor: David Giles
Production editor: John Fremont
Cover design: Chuck Hathaway
Production house: Comp-Type, Inc.
Editorial consultant: William M. Holden
Editorial assistants: Jennifer Kulmann and Linda Gatter

Library of Congress Catalog Card No: 90-084552
ISBN number 0-9627680-7-3

Cox, Leona Dixon. Single Woman Homesteader.
    Primary subjects: Northern California History, Homesteading, Women's resourcefulness, Nature, Wilderness, Home construction.

Printed on recycled paper.
Manufactured in the United States of America.
First edition.

SINGLE WOMAN HOMESTEADER

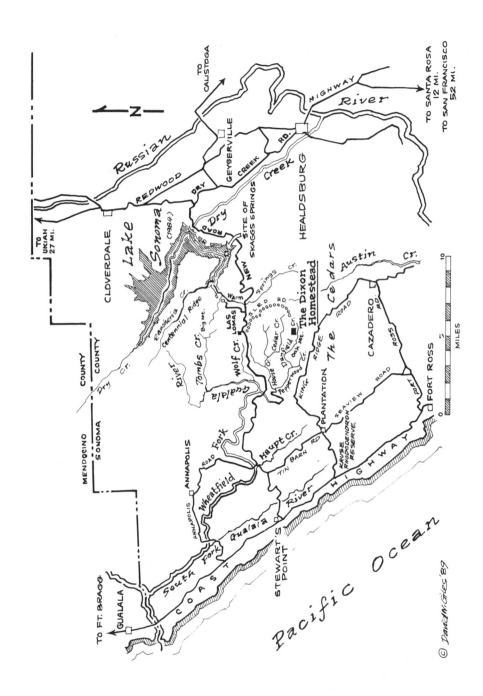

Northwestern Sonoma County

PUTTING IT IN PERSPECTIVE

Sonoma Valley—where Leona Dixon Cox would later establish her homestead—was settled by the Chocuyen Indians until the founding of Sonoma Mission, originally called San Francisco de Solano, in 1819 by Father Jose Altimira. He bestowed the Indian word, Sonoma, meaning "valley of the moon," upon the local chief's people and henceforth both the Indians and mission were known as Sonoma.

In this region of four great valleys and of the Sonoma, Petaluma, Gualala and Russian Rivers, many smaller valleys hide among the coastal mountains. Much of the land is precipitous, descending from Geyser Peak at 3,470 feet through rolling hills to sea level at the Pacific shore. Hot springs erupt throughout the county, notably at The Geysers, which have been attracting health-seekers from throughout the U.S. and Europe since the 1870s.

The climate is generally mild, with a rainfall of 16 inches, somewhat greater than that of San Francisco fifty miles to the southeast.

Fort Ross, a coastal station for supplying provisions to the Russian fur empire, was established in 1812 by the Russian American Trading Company. After Mexico gained independence from Spain in 1822, California came under Mexican jurisdiction. To prevent the encroachment of Russians inland, a young Mexican general of twenty-five, Mariano G. Vallejo, was dispatched with a garrison to Sonoma in 1833. He established Pueblo Sonoma on the site of the original mission, which had been burned out and destroyed in 1823. Other Mexican families followed, received land grants from the Mexican government and became known to history as the Californios. One of these, Dona Maria Ignacia Lopez de Carrillo, widowed with twelve children, was deeded Rancho Cabeza de Santa Rosa. She built the first non-Indian residence in 1837, known as the Carrillo Adobe. One of Dona Lopez de Carrillo's daughters, Francesca Benecia, became the wife of General Vallejo.

By the 1840s, an influx of adventurers, including Captain Johann Sutter, forsook overcrowded and economically distressed conditions or personal disgrace in Europe and South America and came to California in search of land and space. Between 1842 and 1846, the United States and Great Britain maintained fleets on the Pacific Ocean, ready to lay claim to California.

U. S. military figures began hoisting American flags and making proclamations at Monterey and elsewhere, claiming California was U.S. territory. A Bear flag was raised in Sonoma by independent militarists on June 14, 1846. The distinguished General Mariano Vallejo and his officers were taken prisoner and hauled off to Sutter's Fort near Sacramento where they were accorded guest privileges by Captain Sutter, a.k.a. Johann Sutter, of aristocrat persuasion.

After war was declared between the U.S. and Mexico, the Stars and Stripes was raised at Monterey on July 10, and the Bear Flag was pulled down at Sonoma. A peaceful settlement with the Mexican Republic over the California issue was ratified by U.S. President James Knox Polk on March 16, 1848, just in time to exploit the recent discovery of gold in California.

Sonoma County enjoyed a brief flurry of gold mining at Eden Valley in 1852 but was spared the ravages and destruction wreaked by argonauts upon other California settlements. Mercury was mined occasionally, but supply and demand usually kept the price too low for serious operation.

As gold fever subsided and railroads stretched across the continent, successful entrepreneurs sought solace and rest from their labors, and a place to spend their material gains in good health and creature comfort. Sonoma County supervisors subsidized a railroad line from Petaluma to Santa Rosa at the end of 1870. By 1872, the San Francisco and North Pacific Railroad steamed north from Marin County to Cloverdale.

Meanwhile, wagon trails were built to the hot springs, first to The Geysers over Hog's Back Ridge from Healdsburg. On May 15, 1861, R. C. Flournoy drove a double team and buggy on the first trip and delivered a female tourist to the new hotel. The mystical and curative properties of hot mineral water and the Mediterranean landscape attracted more and more tourists to The Geysers. Writers and lecturers spread word of the marvels of Sonoma across continent and seas. Skaggs Springs, eight miles west of the SFNPR depot at Geyserville, offered luxurious warm sulphur springs bathing, with nearby cold iron springs for the restoration of invalids; Lytton Springs provided seltzer water. All the springs were situated in magnificent landscapes. Luxury, health, pleasing vistas and self-indulgence brought fashionable crowds to Sonoma watering places.

Sonoma County's growing reputation for mystical geological properties also attracted spiritualists and Utopians. The Fountain Grove community, organized by Thomas Harriston of London, began in Santa Rosa and attracted a Japanese scholar, Kaynaye Nagawawa, of the noble Satsuma clan, who eventually established a winery there.

French speaking socialists reigned from 1881 to 1887. Readers of William Dean Howells' novel, *A Traveler from Alturia*, gathered in 1894. Unitarians also settled in Sonoma, and a Madame Preston applied her healing skills from 1880 until her death in 1907.

The wines of California probably originated with grapes brought from Spain by mission fathers, but serious viticulture began in Sonoma with a Hungarian noble, Colonel Agoston Haraszthy, arriving by way of Wisconsin in 1856. Publication in 1858 of his *Grape Culture, Wines and Wine-Making*, led to his appointment by Governor John G. Downey as Commissioner to visit wine makers of Europe. He returned with 300 varieties of grape that would be established throughout California.

Before the turn of the century, several luminaries of Sonoma County history took up residence, winning fame or notoriety. Luther Burbank, plant experimenter, moved to

Santa Rosa in 1875 to seek better climate and soil than he had found in his home of Lancaster, Massachusetts. At Santa Rosa, he developed new varieties of potatoes, plums, apples, roses, and a four-inch-diameter Shasta daisy.

Robert Louis Stevenson, suffering from tuberculosis, sought the cures of Sonoma County spas during his 1887-1889 American visit. *The Silverado Squatters*, published in 1883, offered his recollections of Sonoma County.

Black Bart also toured Sonoma County and elsewhere in the west as "poet laureate" and stage coach robber. He traveled without ammunition in his double-barreled shotgun, and left his victims with a poem as well as their lives. A famous hold-up took place on the coast run out of Healdsburg on August 8, 1877.

Following the precedent set for literary pursuits as well as for experimental farming, in 1910 Jack London of San Francisco settled at the Beauty Ranch in Glen Ellen, where he drank, raised pigs and wrote. Another distinguished author, Jessamyn West, settled in Sonoma County with her husband, Harry Maxwell McPherson, a Napa Valley College educator.

Among cosmopolitan settlers attracted to Sonoma County during its first forty years of emigrant settlers was Charles Henry Dixon, the father of Leona Dixon Cox.

The earthquake and subsequent fire of 1906, which destroyed San Francisco, struck with even greater force in Santa Rosa, a fact not generally known. In Sonoma County, one effect at the Las Lomas Ranch was to eliminate a spring of fresh water. The owner, believing his water supply to be gone forever, sold out at a bargain price. Leona's father took over the mortgage—and developed new springs.

CHAPTER 1

CROSSING THE PLAINS

My father's parents, Martha and Alfred Dixon, left Indiana as a very young couple in 1860 with two-year-old William and a six-month-old baby, my father, Charles Henry Dixon. They joined a large train of other four-horse teams at Independence, Missouri, with a big covered wagon that held all their possessions. Some families had milk cows tied to their wagons. Two wagons were pulled by oxen.

They left Independence on April 15, 1861 and traveled about fifteen miles a day. Even on Sundays the teams were hooked up and driven for six or eight miles, to keep the stock from resting too long and growing stiff.

Martha and Alfred Dixon were headed for Elk Grove, about fifteen miles south of Sacramento, where Alfred's father, my great-grandfather, owned a 640 acre wheat ranch. No Indians raided and no major problems slowed their progress.

By October first their wagon train crossed the Sierra Nevada summit at Donner Pass, where the Donner party had foundered in the blizzard of 1846. The Dixons met no severe storms even though winter was close. They arrived at Elk Grove on October 15th and celebrated Dad's first birthday there on November 22, 1861.

I remember that ranch from many Christmases spent there with Uncle Will, Aunt Julia, and their eight children.

Dad and his brother Will learned to drive a plow team

while my grandfather sat in the kitchen reading law books. It seemed to Charles and Will that they were always working.

When grandfather died, Uncle William and my father became partners and sowed wheat every year. They plowed about two-thirds by walking plow and four horses and later got a gang plow with eight horses and rode.

William married Julia Barns and Charles, my future father, married her sister, Jennie Barns, my mother. Charles and Jennie owned a house in Elk Grove when they were first married, and there Jennie gave birth to my two brothers, Harold and Walter.

Dad suffered from asthma and malaria and finally decided to get out of the Sacramento valley. He hitched one of the horses to a buggy and drove to Santa Rosa, where he bought a ten acre prune ranch two miles west of town. It had a very nice house on it and was not far from a good grammar school.

Will bought out Dad's share of the Elk Grove property. Dad rented a box car on the railroad and loaded everything, including Harold's little Indian pony, into it to ship to Santa Rosa. My twin sister, Winona, and I were born there on January 5, 1902.

Dad's asthma continued to bother him. A friend in real estate, Frank Leppo, told him that sometimes a higher altitude helped a person with asthma. He mentioned a mountain ranch Dad might be interested in buying.

Right after the 1906 earthquake, they drove up to look at the Las Lomas ranch, at 1920 feet elevation. A Mr. Spotswood who owned it thought the ranch was ruined because the spring that fed the house had gone dry. Dad didn't think that would make any difference, as there were three more springs up the road, so he bought it.

Dad's asthma never seriously flared up again after we moved to Las Lomas, and in the fresh air wafted in by ocean breezes his malaria disappeared.

The Las Lomas house was originally a hunting lodge built of one- by-twelve redwood boards with battens over the

Las Lomas Rancho

joints and a commercial redwood shingle roof. It was sixty feet square, had a ten-foot porch around it, and sat on 1,983 acres.

Nearly all the adjoining ranches were large. The Sol Walters ranch northwest of us had about 3,000 acres, and ran sheep and cattle. The Bank ranch to the west consisted of 5,000 acres. Bob Caughey raised sheep on it for years on a lease basis. The Colonel Miles ranch joined ours on the east. It ran down across Warm Spring Creek up to the George Shuhart homestead of 160 acres and 100 head of sheep.

South of the Shuhart place, Butch and Maude Waltze owned a cattle ranch for many years, and southwest of their ranch stretched the Old Beard ranch of 1,800 acres. Later it belonged to George and Lute Eachle, then Rose McPherson. Bob McCaughey also ran sheep on it for several years. It bordered the east boundary of the Bank ranch.

To the north of the Shuhart homestead lay the White Oak Ranch now owned by Tom Baxter.

Along Warm Spring Creek were several small places of forty acres each. A bridge crossed Wildcattle Creek where it flowed into Warm Spring at the foot of Las Lomas grade. Harley Groves' house stood west of the road. He was state game warden for years in this area and his ranch had about 800 acres.

A mile down the same road lay the Waltenspiel ranch, with 160 acres. To the north, the Duke Blair ranch ran thousands of acres of sheep.

The Skaggs Springs-Stewarts Point road headed up the canyon past the White Oak ranch buildings, on past the Waltenspiels, the Groves' house and Las Lomas. It ran through the Kashi Indian Reservation and connected with the coast road at Stewart's Point.

The Skaggs Springs resort bordered this road, about three miles from the present overlook point of Lake Sonoma. The resort was built sometime in late 1889, soon after completion of the Northwestern railroad to Geyserville. Around 1900, a family by the name of Curtis bought it and a son, Leo Curtis, inherited it. Before Lake Sonoma Dam was finished, the hotel burned down and was not replaced, for the lake would soon inundate the property anyway.

Skaggs Springs was a popular place, for it had the only post office within twenty miles. It had a dance pavilion and cottages along the mineral spring creek. Crowds of some 300 people swarmed in during the Fourth of July. The Curtises built a wooden dam across Warm Spring Creek for boating in the summer, and James Burgett of Healdsburg constructed a concrete swimming pool.

To get mail, we had to ride horseback or drive ten miles to Skaggs Springs Post Office. The next post office was at Annapolis, eight miles northwest across a steel bridge on the Gualala River. Tons of apples were trucked out from Annapolis from about 1918 on. The Ohlsen brothers had 100 acres of orchard near Annapolis. They bought one of the first trucks, a two-ton Republic with solid rubber tires, and drove it for a good many years. Ed, the oldest of four sons, did all the hauling. The Rasmussen family hauled apples on a smaller Chevrolet truck and the Patchets had their own fruit drier.

I loved our ranch. Winona and I grew up there from the time we were ten years old and in third grade. Mother enrolled us in the Warm Spring Grammar School, four-and-a-half miles down the road towards Healdsburg.

The day Mother enrolled us in school she drove us down with a team of horses in a two-seated surrey. She tied the horses to a tree and we walked up the hill to the school. We were greeted by the teacher, Helen Young from Healdsburg.

Two boys were sitting together. One reached up to the top of his closely cropped head and picked something off with his fingers. He shoved it over in front of the other boy. They both had big grins on their faces. Oh my goodness, I thought, head lice! No. The boy put his find on the floor and ground the life out of it with his boot heel. I later met up with plenty of the same creatures—wood ticks.

The first year we walked the four-and-a-half miles to school every day, and our brother Walter arrived on Peanuts, a small saddle horse, to pick us up when school was over. We rode double and he walked. Our tiny one-room school had one teacher and eight students. They were glad to have us, since it took an attendance of seven to operate a public school. We had a different teacher nearly every year for the pay was low, and hardships were many. Teachers boarded with the nearest neighbor, as a rule, and hiked three miles to the schoolhouse.

The school building was built of rough two-by-four redwood with no finish on the inside. We had twelve desks, a rolltop desk and chair for the teacher, wood heat and a water bucket on a bench with a drinking dipper hanging from a nail.

One day the boys filled the teacher's desk drawer with little green frogs, and when she opened the drawer they all jumped out. She screamed, but no one was punished.

During recess and at noon, we played games: hide-and-go-seek, stealing sticks, dare-base, and a form of baseball. We never had enough players to make regular teams. The pupils either walked to school or were lucky enough to have horses or mules, maybe a Shetland pony or a bicycle, to ride. Winona and I really enjoyed our little mountain school. After the first year we rode Peanuts to school by ourselves, and thereafter we each had a horse of our own. On the way we would visit the little birds that built their nests in moss-covered roots in the high-cut banks of the road. By the time the mother bird had hatched her eggs she was so tame we could stop by the nest and feed her and her babies crumbs from our lunch pails.

From about 1914 to 1918, the neighborhood held a party and dance once a month. Three ranches had living rooms large enough for dances: Our Las Lomas, Harley Groves and the White Oak Ranch owned by Edward van Dyke. The dances lasted all night as nearly everyone came a great distance by horse and buggy, or teams and spring wagons. Friends from Dry Creek drove Model T Fords: George and Molly Somes came with Phillip and Ruth, and George Bell with his wife and children, Duvall, Walter and Rowena. George Bell and George Somes had prune ranches in upper

Livingroom of Las Lomas Ranch house

Dry Creek. The two Georges later bought the Shuhart homestead from Effie after her husband passed away.

We danced fox trots, three-step waltzes, two-steps and occasionally a Virginia reel, to the music of cylinder recordings on the Edison phonograph, and also flat records played on a Victrola. No one in the neighborhood played accordion or violin. There were games for the children: musical chairs, spin-the-plate and drop-the-handkerchief. The van Dyke boys, John, Bob and Ned, loved to play with matches. Fortunately, someone always rushed to the scene before one of their fires did real damage.

Harley Groves, the gamewarden, came with May and their three boys, Edwin, Lawrence and Orland. Orly was the clown at our grammar school.

Our mother, Jennie, often made up skits about people in the neighborhood and kept everyone in stitches as she recited them. Sometimes she passed out scripts so people could read their own lines.

As night drew on, the children fell asleep and were put to bed. A potluck meal was served at midnight and friends and neighbors visited and danced until nearly daylight, at which time breakfast was served.

My twin sister Winona just loved cooking, keeping house, sewing and all domestic work, whereas I couldn't get out of the house fast enough after breakfast, so I became Dad's right-hand helper. Winona and I helped round up the cattle, and I learned to build fence, cut wood and brush, and when I grew older I helped shoe the horses.

All told, we rode enough miles to grammar school to ride across the United States and back again. When we graduated, the folks were not financially able to board us out in Healdsburg for high school, so we had to spend an extra year in grammar school. The next year we stayed out of school; then, in 1918, Mother took the job of cook in the high school cafeteria. We rented a small house, and Mother, Winona and I moved to Healdsburg but spent all our vacations on the ranch.

In 1915, Mother took Winona and me to San Francisco to visit the Panama-Pacific World's Fair and Exposition. I vividly remember the beautiful Palace of Fine Arts designed by Maybeck. I was captivated by the Hawaiian music, which I believe was played there for the first time. I'll never forget how excited we were with that strange, new music.

My older brother, Harold, came back to the ranch with his wife and daughter while Winona and I were in town with Mother, but they soon left because there was not enough money to be made on the ranch.

In the summer of 1921, Mother had her first stroke. Winona took care of her at the ranch and I took a job as receptionist for Dr. Kinley, the dentist, and F.E. Sohlor, M.D., in Healdsburg. When hunting season came around, the first day of August, I quit town and went back to the ranch to guide the hunters who came each year. I thoroughly disliked office work. I made my mind up I would never work in town. I wanted my own ranch with cattle or sheep, or both.

At the first of the next term, I explained our situation to the school superintendent, Mr. Morehead, and got his permission to take our books home to study and then come back for examinations. Winona and I graduated with our class in 1922.

Walter and Maude and their family moved back to Las Lomas from Humboldt County in 1923 to help Dad. Las Lomas had quite a lot of redwood timber so Walter began working it into split items, grape stakes, railroad ties and posts.

One day a tall young man with square-shoulders and sparkling blue eyes rode into the ranch on a fine bay. He was Elbert White from Connecticut, and he had heard in Europe about a Cloverdale homestead from a fellow marine named Mansfield. After the war and after working for other ranches, Elbert filed on a 640-acre grazing homestead. His land was several miles north of Las Lomas. He did well as a sheep rancher and was back to visit quite often. He and Winona married in April of 1926.

We had a staggering blow in March of 1926—Las Lomas

caught fire and burned to the ground. We lost the house and contents, including Walter's furniture and all the records of the hunters who had come to the lodge each fall. Walter moved his family to Santa Rosa to live with Maude's mother on her five-acre place, and commuted every day to the ranch in a Model T.

We hired a couple of carpenters for two weeks to lay foundation and do the framing for the new house, then Walter and I went right to work and rebuilt it, using the same floor plan. We spent the whole summer siding, roofing, and finishing the inside with plasterboard and paint, instead of working in the woods to solve our cash-flow problem, which was becoming serious.

Elbert and Winona leased the Las Lomas ranch range and moved into Walter's homestead cabin. Elbert brought his sheep along, and bought more to put on the range. After deer season that year they moved into one of the hunters' cabins across the road. Winona was still caring for Mother during the day, and I attended her through the night.

Dad once told me he thought Mother's and his biggest mistake in life was not taking their cash and paying for the ranch. They bought stock in a coal mine instead and eventually lost it all. Dad thought the worry of where the next dollar was coming from, to meet mortgage payments, or pay taxes, or buy feed, had a lot to do with Mother's sickness. After a series of strokes, she died on July 20, 1928 at age 62.

Elbert's experience with his homestead gave me the inspiration to file on 640 acres of my own west of Las Lomas. I had worked right along with Walter in the timber, and knew how to split shakes and boards when it came time to build my own cabin. The time came soon enough. Walter and I watched the economy fail after the Crash of 1929, and by 1932 we realized the ranch would soon be lost. My 640 acres of untouched wilderness stood ready as the economy worsened.

CHAPTER 2

LOCATING THE PROPERTY

"We simply can't go on this way," I said to Walter and my father. We sat on the wide front porch of our Las Lomas ranch house. The big June moon was rising over the east ridge and a slight breeze stirred the leaves on the tan oak by the corner of the porch.

"Last year wool brought sixty cents a pound," I continued. "This year the same fleece of wool is only worth three cents."

Our ewes averaged seven pounds of wool apiece. Lambs were the same. The year before, a sixty-five pound average lamb, live weight, brought fifteen cents per pound, or $9.75. This year the same lamb brought $1.95. "The cost of shearing has to come out of this," I said. "There is no way in the world we can meet mortgage payments twice a year, or insurance payments or property taxes. Besides we all have to have living expenses."

The Great Depression which followed the stock market crash of 1929 had come between us and the peace and tranquility of the evening. Values had plummeted. Everyone was affected.

Our father, Charles Henry Dixon, was in his early 70s and failing in health, though he still stood over six feet tall, straight and slender. Our dear mother, Jennie Lavinia Barnes Dixon, had passed away in 1928 after a long illness.

As Dad's strength waned, he had turned Las Lomas over to Walter and me. Now we faced the dilemma of running a 2,000 acre stock ranch without operating funds. As the

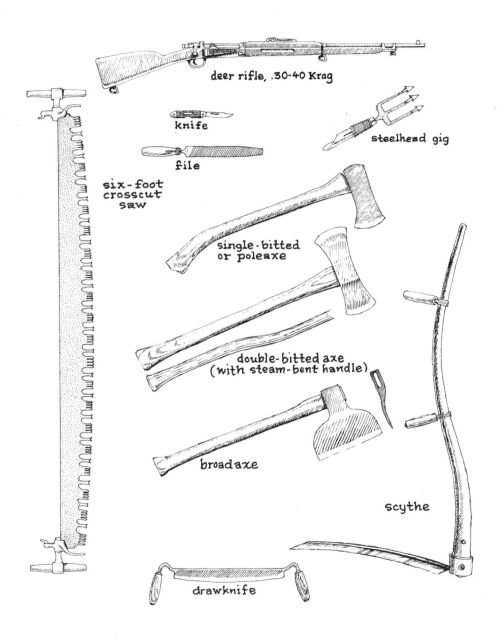

deer rifle, .30-40 Krag

knife

file

steelhead gig

six-foot
crosscut
saw

single-bitted
or poleaxe

double-bitted axe
(with steam-bent handle)

broadaxe

scythe

drawknife

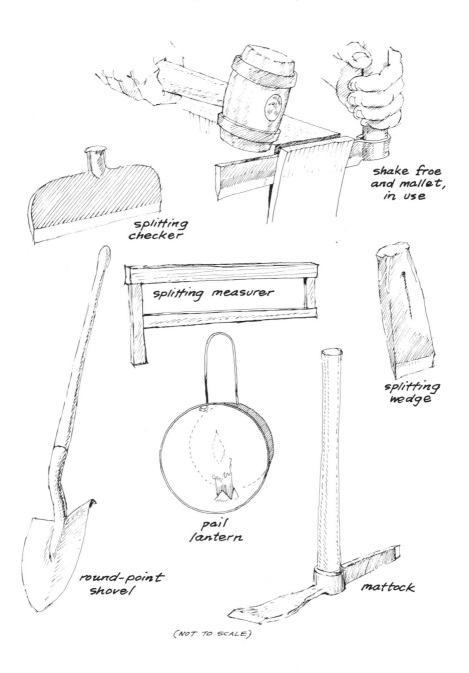

shake froe
and mallet,
in use

splitting
checker

splitting measurer

splitting
wedge

pail
lantern

round-point
shovel

mattock

(NOT TO SCALE)

economy began to fail, we borrowed money to buy stock. Now our wool, sheep and other stock could not cover the costs of feed and maintenance.

My brother was the image of his father in his younger days. He had brown hair and dark brown eyes, whereas Dad's full head of hair was now salt and pepper. Walter always wore Levi jeans and boots and a regular blue chambray shirt. After graduating from grammar school, he had worked three years on the ranch, then attended Sweet's Business College in Santa Rosa.

I took after my mother's side of the family, with light blonde hair and light blue-gray eyes. I, too, was rather tall, five foot seven-and-a-half inches, slender, and very strong and muscular from doing nearly all the outside work on the ranch.

My twin sister, Winona, not identical in the least, had dark brown hair and was five inches shorter. We never cared for the same things; she liked everything pertaining to the house, and was a wonderful seamstress and housekeeper. Her husband, Elbert, was still a sheep rancher.

Dad thought about my question and finally answered. "That's right, Leona. With mortgage payments twice a year, taxes to pay and house insurance, something has to be done."

Walter and his family lived in Santa Rosa. When Maude's mother, Mina Huckaby, passed on, she willed them her home. Now Walter and Maude had a secure home, Walter having helped his mother-in-law pay off her mortgage. Walter had filed on a 640-acre homestead and I had helped him build a cabin on 120 acres that lay inside the boundary of the Las Lomas ranch.

I said, "If we sell the ranch, you will still have the 520 acres adjoining my 640 acres that you have already filed on. You no doubt will sell the 120 acres that lie within the Las Lomas Ranch." A person could file on two separate parcels of land within twenty air miles. "I think we should give serious thought to the couple who are interested in buying this place."

"They don't want to pay anything above the existing mortgage for it," Walter said.

"I don't think we have much choice," I said. "When you go home this Friday, you'd better contact them again."

I turned to my father. "Dad, do you think you and I can get a cabin built on my land and move there before the winter sets in?"

"I'll do all I'm able, but you know I'm no carpenter."

"Oh, piffle. We'll get by some way."

That was the beginning of a plan which would carry us through the Depression. During the next five years we enjoyed the comfort of a sturdy cabin, plentiful game and a fine garden, all with a cash outlay of only five dollars.

Walter walked in early one evening as I was cooking supper. "Leona," he said, "We'd better think about locating your 640 acres and my 520 acres. How about riding over there tomorrow?"

The next morning after an early breakfast, Walter went down to the barn and saddled Peanuts for himself and Bell for me. I washed the dishes, put up a lunch and straightened the house. Dad said he would stay at home and cut wood.

Walter led the horses up from the barn. We mounted and rode up the old sled road that wound around the small fir-timbered mountain in front of the house. The road was not wide enough to drive a wagon or a car on. It followed a long ridge for three miles and ended at the old abandoned Smith orchard. While Walter was still living on the Las Lomas ranch he worked for Bob Caughey who rented the 5,000 acres of the Smith place and ran sheep on it. One year he had Walter pick the prunes. He dried them in the orchard, then boxed them and hauled them out with one of Dad's sleds to the road at Las Lomas to be picked up by truck. The sled runners were cut out of a six- or eight-inch limb six feet long with a natural up-curve on the front to keep the runners from digging into the ground. These runners were so shiny and smooth that Walter would have to put a heavy chain around the runners

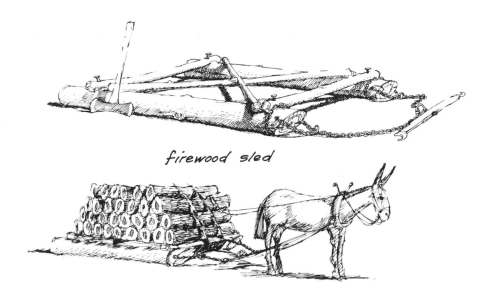

firewood sled

when going down a steep hill to hold the sled back, so it wouldn't run over the horses.

Walter opened the gate in the dividing fence between Las Lomas and the Bank ranch and we rode through. The old sled road followed the top of a long ridge through patches of nice black oak timber and a lot of open country. As we rode out past the abandoned Smith orchard, we saw lots of deer. They loved to feed on the fruit that fell off the trees, but when we appeared they ran off in all directions.

Walter had worked with a survey crew through the previous summer, surveying the boundary of the Bank ranch so he knew where some of the corners were. He said, "Leona, we'll ride down off the end of this ridge and find a different kind of timber. Every rancher I know calls them cedar trees. I think your northeast corner should be on this side of them."

We hunted all around but could find nothing. Walter decided the best thing to do was ride back to the ranch and figure out how to find a corner.

That same evening we were out on the porch again. Katydids were singing their evening songs and fireflies were thick on the lawn. I often marveled that they always carried a little light with them. As usual a slight breeze was creating a nice stir of air.

Walter said, "I know where there's a section corner on the north side of Hazel Hill. We rode by it today. We could start there and survey a line due south, sixteen degrees east, and maybe come close enough to find your section corner."

"That would be roughly about two miles wouldn't it, Walter?" I asked.

"Yes. It's a long line to survey, especially when all we really have is a good compass. I have all the maps marked with the section corners. Our problem is to find them."

I said, "I know a line has to be level. Do you suppose we could use the rawhide braided lariat to measure with, and the small carpenter's level we have, and get close enough to find the corners?"

"That's a possibility, and we might just have to do it that way."

"It'll be a big job, Walter, but nothing comes easy."

"It would be much easier if we had a transit and a rod to measure with, but we don't. Let's start on it the first of next week, Leona."

"That's fine with me."

Walter and I marked feet on the lariat with adhesive tape.

Next Monday morning, I put up a lunch, gathered our meager surveying tools together and as soon as Walter drove in from Santa Rosa we were ready to go.

We rode our horses over to Hazel Hill, dismounted and tied each to a tree. The woods were fresh and damp in the cool morning. Several deer were out feeding and we saw one fine buck.

We walked over to the survey corner—a pile of rock two feet high and three feet square with a short redwood post set in the center. The post had the section corner numbers chiseled into it. Walter drove a nail into the top of the post and placed the small loop of the end of the lariat over it. I took hold of the lariat and walked out, while Walter directed, left or right, according to his compass reading. We were running a line sixteen degrees east going south. I could walk only so far, as the lariat had to be pulled tight and level in order to accurately measure the number of feet. Since we were on a downward slope, soon the rope would be over my head. To give me a starting point for each measure, I dropped a pebble to the ground from the end of the lariat. I recorded each measurement in my notebook. I carried a few pebbles in my pocket and a couple of stakes and drove one in where each pebble hit the ground. That gave me something to loop the lariat over to start the next measure.

It was slow, but as we went along we found some old slash marks where brush had been cut and presumed it was an old survey line. It was time to quit for the day before we got far enough to find a corner.

Late the next day we found a corner, which meant we had gone exactly one mile. Walter was so elated, he whooped and hollered, "We did it Leona! It's working. We've found a corner!"

"Not bad *and* hurray for us," I hollered. This gave us a lot of encouragement. There is a built-up corner, usually made of rocks, on every section corner which marks one mile. The original United States government surveyors wrote the field notes for every corner when this land was first surveyed, beginning about 1876.

In the evening we rested in our favorite place on the porch at Las Lomas. It was very quiet with only a slight breeze blowing across the porch. Suddenly, a big horned owl gave his evening hoot up on the mountain across the road.

Dad asked, "How're you doing with the survey?"

"It went well today," Walter said. "From now on it'll take more time. There's a lot of brush to cut to get a line in there, and it's much steeper country."

The mountain we were surveying was a very rocky one covered with small cedar trees so thick a person had to bend them sideways to walk through. We kept at the job every day that week, and by Friday afternoon we thought we should be close to finding another corner of my property. Walter and I hacked through the brush in a circle and kept enlarging the circles and by jingo, we found it!

The corner was a pile of rock, its location corresponding to the section corner numbers in the government surveyor's field notes, which also indicated the number of feet to a witness tree. We found the tree, identifying it by the distinctive old blaze mark it still bore. Under the bark the same marks would be chiseled into the wood that were on the post in the pile of rock. If the bark was chopped off they would be plain to read. Blazing was done by the original surveyors, and is a backup in case the corner is destroyed by someone or the post is burned or rotted away.

We had done a lot of hard work to find this marker, and to say that Walter and I were happy would be putting it mildly. By sighting a compass line running west, estimating one mile, and sighting another running south one mile, we had a good idea where I could build a cabin that was sure to be on my property.

In some cases corners have been destroyed and the surveyor has to find witness trees, some of which may disappear with the passage of time. Witness tree locations are contained in the field notes for every corner. If there are no trees in the vicinity, the site is marked by rocks placed so many feet away from the actual corner. Any person may obtain field notes for whatever section he is interested in by contacting a government patent office.

A Congressional enactment of 1862 provided a settler with 160 acres of free public land for cultivation and improvement and eventual ownership. Much later, in 1916, the Grazing Homestead Act was enacted. This offered a settler 640 acres with the same stipulation to improve the land to receive the patent to it.

Work to satisfy the requirements might include building a cabin, fencing, brush cutting or clearing land and building trails. A person had five years to do the improvement work on his homestead in order to receive the patent to it from the government. A government agent would inspect the homestead to see if the improvement work had been done. There were no taxes to pay until one received the patent to the land which is signed by the President of the United States. The patent to my 640 acres was signed by President Franklin Delano Roosevelt in 1938.

I know of several instances where a cabin was not built on the filed land. In one case, Mr. Con Orr filed on a homestead in 1927, packed finished lumber in on his back and built a two-room cabin. Two years later he had some of his boundary lines surveyed—and found out his cabin was almost a half mile off his property! He was so disgusted he packed up some personal things and took off for good.

Years later, I bought the land the cabin was on, rebuilt the cabin and lived in it.

CHAPTER 3

THE CABIN SITE

In early August 1932, my brother walked into the house and said, "Leona, time's getting short. We'd better go over to your homestead and try to find a good spring and a place to build your cabin."

"Do you have anything planned for tomorrow, Walter?"

"Not really."

"Then let's take a ride. Why don't we camp out a night or two? We might try deer hunting."

"That's a good idea, Leona."

Dean, Walter's son, rushed in the door. He was twelve years old, a little short for his age, with light brown hair streaked from the summer sun. He had a lot of energy and big blue eyes that took in everything; he could spot a deer a quarter of a mile away, and had already killed his first two bucks.

He evidently had overheard some of our conversation. "Where you going? Can I go too? You going hunting?"

"Hey, wait a minute," his Dad said. "One thing at a time. Yes, you may go. We're going to Aunt Leona's homestead and find a nice place to build her cabin. We also might find out how good the deer hunting is."

Dean jumped up and down: "Can we get enough deer meat so Aunt Nono and I can make some jerky? You know how much I like jerky!"

"Good land, yes!" I replied. "I never can get enough to fill you up."

His Dad said, "Depends a lot on the hunter, Dean. First, he has to *find* the bucks, then get off a good shot or two. He can't get buck fever and expect to get a buck."

"Yeah, I know, Dad."

"First things first. Now you can run errands for Aunt Nono and help her get everything together. After that, go down to the barn and measure out grain for three saddle horses—four gallon cans of rolled barley to a sack. You'll need three sacks. Bring them up here to the house. The horses won't have any hay until they get back here but we might find some good grass they can graze on."

I started to get some cooking pots and dishes together. First I took a two-pound coffee can out to the chopping block and punched two holes in it under the rim, and cut a piece of wire. Baling wire held many things together on the old western ranches, and now it made a handle for my coffee pot, so I could hang it over the camp fire.

I packed the canned goods in flour sacks. Butter, cream and anything perishable would wait until morning. I'd pack the butter in a small glass jar, and cream in another. I put in a jar of wild honey that Walter had robbed from a bee tree late last fall. I made up three bedrolls of blankets and placed everything in a pile by the front door of the living room, ready to be packed on the horses in the morning.

My little bay mare was named Betty. Walter and Dean had two mares a little larger. Walter's was a bay named Babe, and Dean's was a black named Bonnie. These two were a driving team. All our saddle horses were broken to the harness.

Early next morning right after breakfast, Walter and Dad brought the horses up from the barn. Dad held them while Dean and I carried the gear out to Walter, and he divided it up for each horse. He tied the bedrolls behind the saddles and hung the sacks, one on each side of the saddle horns, so we could all ride our horses.

"Get your rifles and we're ready to go," Walter said. We picked up our rifles and shoved them into the leather scabbards on the saddles, then swung up into our saddles. By this time it was only six-thirty in the morning.

"We'll be back in three days, Dad. Take care," Walter said.

"Bye, Dad," I hollered, as my horse whirled around, eager to be gone.

"Good bye, Granddad," Dean hollered.

"Have a good time," Dad said, "and I hope you bring back some nice meat."

For the first three miles we followed the old sled road out past the Smith orchard. As it was early, we saw deer along the side of the road. When we rode past the orchard, we stopped to count them as they went trotting off over the hill.

"I counted twenty-five," Walter said. "There were some nice bucks in the bunch, too."

"Why didn't you shoot one, Dad?" Dean asked.

"We don't want one *now*!"

"Maybe we'll find some down on my claim," I said.

This old orchard had been abandoned many years ago. A man by the name of Frank Fry had taken up a grazing homestead beyond the old orchard and had extended the road down to his cabin. He worked on the sled road with a pick and shovel until he could drive his old pickup over it. After the road passed the orchard, it ran over the end of the ridge and down to a divide. It was very steep.

Frank liked to drink occasionally, and if he ran off that road once, I'll bet he ran that old pickup over the bank a dozen times. One time he didn't pick a good spot when he rolled it, and he came out with a broken arm. That never stopped him though, neither the drinking nor the driving.

We rode down to the divide. Frank Fry's road turned off to the left and it was only a little way to his cabin.

There was a trail here, marked on the maps as "The Old Government Trail." It was opened up by the United States government surveyors when this land was first surveyed. It started out of Healdsburg and headed up Mill Creek, mostly west. It ran up over the Mill Creek summit, which was always known as the Ladder.

This trail, used by the Kashia Indian tribe in early years, was very deeply rutted in places. We picked up the trail and followed it until we came to a blazed trail that turned to the left and started up over the mountain. This was above the corner that we had found when we surveyed. Walter and I had looked for water on the north side of this mountain when we found my corner but never found any.

Now we decided to follow this trail. It was so overgrown with small cedars that we had to dismount and use our axes to get through. "Walter," I said, "have you ever seen anything like this before?"

"Gosh no! This stuff is as thick as the hair on a dog's back. Limbs are tight and stiff and start to grow right out of the trunk at ground level."

Walter and I kept chopping. Dean was trying to throw the small trees out over the trees along the trail. Dean finally said, "Gee, Dad, how long do we have to chop brush?"

"How do I know? I guess until we reach the top of the mountain."

Sure enough, when we came out on top there was a nice big opening. While we rested on top of the mountain, we decided the mountain must have been covered with big trees at one time. Then a big hot forest fire burned all the trees. After a hot fire, the seeds from the cones drop into the ashes and I think, in this case, every seed had sprouted.

We had worked up a pretty good sweat getting rid of all the trees. "Let's have a drink," Walter said to Dean.

The canteen was hanging on the saddlehorn of one of the horses. Dean handed it to me and I took a swallow. "Wow, that's not just warm, that's almost hot," I said and handed it to Walter.

He took a big swig and said, "Well, I certainly have had better things to drink, but at least it wets one's whistle."

"I do hope the going will be better down the other side of the mountain," Walter said.

"Let's get started."

Dean piped up, "Yeah, I could sure use a cool drink."

CHAPTER 4

SURPRISE! SURPRISE!

It had taken over three hours to chop our way through the tangle of trees and get to the top of the mountain. Traveling down the west side of the mountain was not bad. The old blaze was easy to follow and the trees were bigger and well spaced with grassy openings here and there amid patches of manzanita and chamise brush.

"Aunt Nono," Dean asked, "do you think this would be good buck country?"

"It certainly looks like it to me."

"I sure would like to see a buck." Just then we heard a big crash in the manzanita patch to the left of us, and there went several deer scampering down towards the bottom of the canyon.

"Hey! Aunt Nono, did you see what they were?"

"No, I just got a glimpse. At least we know there are deer in here."

There was quite a canyon on the south side of us, beautiful but rough and rugged. The top part was covered with brush, but lower down we could see big cedar trees, then a rocky, bench-like ridge running down into the creek bottom.

Walter stopped. "Look at that country, Leona, it looks like a hunter's paradise."

"Man! It sure does."

We made a turn in the trail and were just above a level plateau about four hundred yards long that sloped up to the top of a mountain. The peak was covered with a heavy

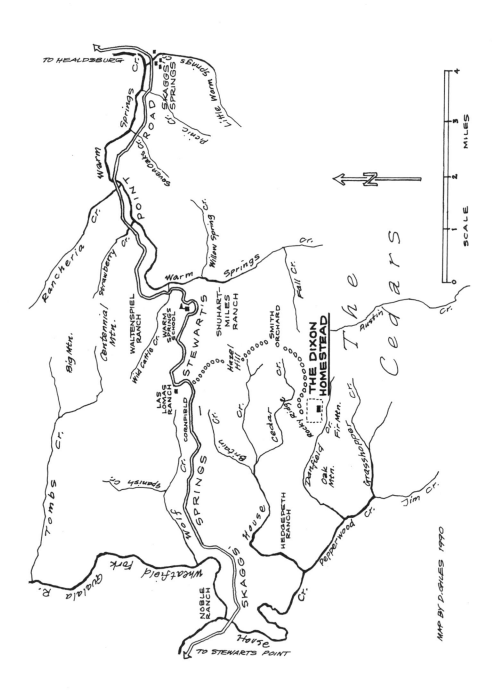

Vicinity of the Homestead

growth of huge Douglas fir and the plateau had a low growth of scrubby manzanita.

"I think we've come far enough," Walter said.

We could hear water running in the canyon to our left. The hillsides to the north of us were covered with oak and fir timber. We presumed there was water in there, too.

"Let's tie our horses here and do a little exploring," Walter said.

We dismounted and let out the cinches so the horses would rest easier.

Walter pulled his maps out of the saddle pocket and studied them. "I think the water we hear must be Danfield Creek, and the one on our north is Cedar Creek. Suppose we separate and look around."

"I'll take my rifle and go out the flat a ways," I said. "I'll look around this small canyon to the right of me for a spring."

"All right," Walter replied. "I'm going around the mountain towards the Danfield."

"Gee, that leaves the north side for me," Dean grumbled.

We pulled our rifles out of our scabbards.

Walter spoke up, "Remember, we're to look for a spring near level ground to build a cabin on. If any one gets a shot at a buck, nail him—we can use the meat."

I said, "Let's meet back here in an hour."

Walter carried a 32 Remington automatic. I had a 25-35 Winchester lever action, and Dean had an 1898 Krag, a rifle from the Spanish-American War.

I walked out the flat ridge a little way. It was covered with scrubby manzanita and all through it was loose, red rock. To me, it looked like Mt. Lassen country, a volcanic formation. The little draw on my right ran down into Cedar Creek. I walked over to the edge and could see almost to the bottom. It was very open and the ground was covered with tall bunch grass.

Gee! I thought, What a place to see a buck. I worked down the hill sideways and back and found a good place to sit down. I had a great view of the hillside across the little canyon. As I sat there I tried to visualize what it would be like to be over in the heavy fir timber on the peak.

I really didn't have much time to think, because I heard a twig snap. There were three deer in single file sneaking up the hillside below me. Holy smoke! They were all bucks.

Gee whiz! I thought, Meat right off the bat! I slowly raised my rifle and pulled the hammer back, took careful aim at the buck in back and squeezed the trigger. I hit him hard and he went down. I quickly pumped another shell into the chamber, aimed at the second one and fired. He dropped right there. I sat still and let the one in front walk on over the ridge. Surely two were enough for Dean's jerky. Needless to say, I'm as bad as he is when it comes to jerky.

Lots of people ask why I shot the ones in back. This doesn't frighten the ones in front. I could have taken all three but I'm not that kind of a hunter. Once, five bucks passed me in single file. I could have taken all of them, but I only wanted a piece of meat, so I took the one in the back of the line and let all the others walk on.

I made my way down to the bucks. They were nice ones, fat and slick. One was a three pointer, western count, and the other a nice forked horn. I rummaged around in the front pocket of my jeans and pulled out my pocket knife, then proceeded to field dress both of them. After I was through I dragged each one under a thick little cedar tree. I wanted them in deep shade until we could load them onto the horses.

I worked my way back up the hill to the horses. By the time I arrived, Walter and Dean were back. They had heard me shoot.

Dean immediately asked, "What did you shoot at?"

"I bet you found a big rattlesnake and shot him," Walter said.

"What! with two shots!" I said. "No, you'll never guess. We certainly won't have to go without meat."

"Gee! Aunt Nono, did you get a big one? Big enough to make jerky?"

"Well, probably. I have two nice big bucks and they're already dressed out, as you can see by my hands."

"Yippee!" Dean yelled.

"Do you have them in the shade?" Walter asked.

"Yes, under thick little cedar trees."

"Well, now that the excitement is over let's get back to looking for the cabin site." Walter said. "I made it around the hill to the banks of Danfield Creek. It's running a nice stream of water. I think we should go look at it."

"Is there enough of a trail to get the horses down?"

"Yes, Leona. There isn't any brush and there's only one rough spot where we have to cross a rocky ridge."

We untied the horses and walked, leading the horses. It was only a short way around the hill to the rocky ridge. When we crossed the ridge, what a sight I looked down upon!

There was a flat area of about an acre or so covered with tall cedar trees and manzanita, open enough we could walk right through. Then up at the other end was a waterfall.

"My goodness, what a sight!" I exclaimed.

We led our horses down into the flat then worked our way between the trees up to the waterfall, which was much bigger than I thought, about fourteen feet high.

"Look at that big pool at the bottom of the falls," Walter said.

"How deep do you think that water is, Dad?"

"How the heck would I know, Dean? Why don't you go jump in? You were complaining about being hot a while ago."

Dean ran over to the pool and put his hands in the water. "Wow! It's too cold for me. It's like ice water."

Walter and I decided this was a good place to make our camp.

We unsaddled the horses and led them down to the stream and let them drink. Walter and Dean then took them up on the flat and tied each one to a tree. We all gathered at the pool and got a drink, then washed our faces. It was cold and refreshing after all the brush chopping we had done to get there. The pool was about sixteen feet across and almost round. Of course with the high falls there was a high bank on three sides of it.

We sat there enjoying the westerly breeze that was softly blowing up the canyon. It was a great place to be. We talked about the creek, the falls, the flat and the trip in.

"I wonder if this wouldn't be the place to build the cabin," I said to Walter.

"It sure does look good. But I think we should look over across the creek where we could see the big trees as we came down the trail," Walter said.

Dean spoke up. "Over in Cedar Creek there was not very much water running, and I didn't find a nice level place like this."

"It would be much better here on the south side of the hill too, as it would be warmer in winter time," Walter said.

"Let's explore all the possibilities," I said.

"I think we should saddle the horses and go pack in your bucks now," Walter said.

"Yeah, let's go," Dean said. "I want to see those bucks."

We saddled the horses and led them over the ridge, then mounted up and rode out to where we first had them tied. It took us almost the rest of the afternoon to get the deer loaded and packed back to the camp site and hung up.

Walter immediately took the livers out of them and I carried them down to the creek and placed them in the running cold water.

While Walter and Dean were skinning the two deer, I built a small fire pit of rock and got a bigger rock to poke my long stick under. I found a forked stick to drive in the ground on the other side of the fire to hold the end of the long coffee pot stick. Now I was ready to cook supper. I started the fire, then washed some potatoes and wrapped them in several thicknesses of wet newspaper. I raked some coals out towards the edge of the fire, laid the wrapped potatoes on top and covered them with hot ashes and dirt. While the potatoes were baking I put coffee in the pot, added the water, and hung it on the pole across the fire.

I ran down to the creek and picked up one of the livers and ran back to the fire, then sliced it on a flat rock I had washed for this purpose. When the boys finished with the deer, I placed the frying pan over the coals, put some butter in the pan, sliced a big onion into it and let it cook a little while. Then I added the liver.

Finally, I spread a blanket out and laid a table cloth over it and we were ready for dinner. The boys went down to the creek to wash and when they came back we sat down to eat. I had homemade bread and butter to go with the liver and onions and baked potatoes. For dessert, we finished off a quart of home canned peaches.

I was thinking about how good the food tasted when I suddenly realized, "You know, we never had any lunch."

"Gee! that's right." Walter said. "I'm surprised at you, Dean, you're always starving to death. How come?"

"Yeah, I forgot all about eating with so much excitement, but now come to think of it, I believe I was almost starved to death."

As it grew dark, the bonfire felt good, the breeze had changed and was coming down the canyon. There was a decided chill in the air. Walter kept the fire burning.

As we lay around the fire, Dean said, "Dad, tell some of your hunting stories."

Walter and I had plenty of them to relate. We took turns, telling funny stories as well as a few hair-raising ones, like the one we always had to tell on Winona's husband, Elbert.

One time Elbert, Winona and I had been out wild hog hunting. As we headed home and it was almost dark, the dogs ran off and bayed down in Big Mountain Creek. We rushed down there on our saddle horses, thinking they had a hog. Well, of all things, they had a forked horn deer bayed by a big patch of woodwardia ferns. We didn't want the deer and Elbert couldn't get the dogs to leave the deer. He jumped down in the creek bed to get closer to the dogs, and the deer charged Elbert.

"Look out!" I yelled.

Just as he put his hands up in front of him, the deer's horns came right into them and shoved him back against the creek bank.

"What am I going to do with him now?" he hollered.

"Shove him into the ferns! I'll get hold of the dogs, then you run for the bank!"

He made it. I got the dogs to quit barking and Elbert scrambled up on the bank, while the deer took off around the fern patch. We mounted our horses (Winona had been holding them) and rode the rest of the way to Las Lomas in the dark.

"Speaking of dark," Walter said, "let's make up our bed rolls and turn in; it's getting chilly."

It has been 56 years since I ate that meal, but I remember it so well, it seems like it was just the other day. I went to sleep listening to the rhythmic, soothing music of the waterfall and the *whoo-whoo-whoo-whoo-whoo* of a big horned owl over in one of the big cedar trees across the creek. It sounded to me like he was saying, "Who are you, who are you?"

The next morning we were up before the sun peeked over the mountain. It was still chilly there by the waterfall. We finished off a great breakfast of homemade, sugar-cured smoked bacon, eggs, coffee and toast made over the coals.

"Come on," Walter said to Dean. "Help me pull the meat sacks up over the deer."

"How did Aunt Nono know to bring two deer sacks?" Dean asked.

"Oh, I guess she had a premonition of what might happen," Walter said.

They soon finished with the deer. "Leona," Walter said, "let's walk up the creek a ways and look around, then cross over and look in the big trees."

"All right, I'll be right with you." Many huge rough boulders, some as big as a house, choked the creek. We crossed over and climbed to the big trees that were spaced a good distance apart. It looked like a park and felt good underfoot as needles lay thick on the ground. Unfortunately, the site was such a steep sidehill that building on it was out of the question.

We walked back to camp, then followed the creek downstream. Past the flat ground the creek margins were so rough we retreated to our campground.

After lunch, we saddled the horses and rode towards Cedar Creek. The brush was so thick we had to stop and tie the horses—near where we had tied them the day before.

Just as Dean had told us, there wasn't much water running in Cedar Creek, and we didn't find any flat ground. The timber was all fir and black oak. We decided the best place to build the cabin was the place we had stumbled onto, the flat on Danfield Creek.

"Yeah, I like the flat and the waterfall and the big pool of water," Dean said.

When we returned to camp, Dean and Walter unsaddled the three horses and fed them their rolled barley. "I guess the horses will be glad to get back to the ranch and get some of that good oat hay," Walter said.

We had another good dinner. While I was doing the dishes, Walter called out: "Come on, Dean, let's take the sacks off the deer, so the cool night air can blow on the meat."

We sat around the fire awhile that evening and talked about where to place the cabin, but soon turned in, as we wanted to get up early and be on our way home before it warmed up.

Walter and I certainly knew a lot more about my claim now. The old horned owl was still talking, or maybe complaining about our intrusion into his domain. The waterfall sang its lullaby. Later I saw the moon looking down upon the quiet wilderness.

Next morning we woke early. Before breakfast, Betty whinnied to Walter for her feed of barley, so he fed all three horses. Dean built a fire and I cooked breakfast.

While I packed up the kitchen things, the boys took the deer down and wrapped them with blankets. Walter packed both of them onto the saddle of his horse, Babe.

We took turns walking and riding the horses, and made good time going home. We didn't have any brush to cut and it didn't seem as far either. The horses were anxious to get back home on the ranch. We arrived before noon and had a lot to tell Dad. He was glad to see all the meat, too.

As we were eating dinner that evening, Dean said, "Gee! that was a good camping trip. Only I wish I could have killed a buck."

"Don't be so impatient, Dean. You have your whole life ahead of you and no doubt a lot of years to hunt," his Dad told him. "Look at your Aunt Nono. She killed her first deer when she was eleven years old, and with my 22 rifle, too. She's never missed a season since, and will probably get her annual two bucks for years to come. She enjoys the outdoors and all the tremendous things that go along with it. I hope you'll grow up and take time to absorb all the good things of nature. Open your eyes and watch the beautiful sunsets. Take time to just sit in the woods and see the wild life around you. That's what hunting trips are all about. Enjoy the great outdoors on every trip you take, big or little."

"Gee Dad, I never looked at it that way—never really thought about it. Guess I'll have a lot of time to hunt. I know a lot of boys aren't lucky enough to have a Dad to take them hunting, and have an Aunt like Aunt Nono."

CHAPTER 5

THE BEGINNING

Walter finally got in touch with the couple that wanted to buy the Las Lomas ranch. "They're still interested," Walter said. "It's nearly the first of September. We'd better get things worked out."

Walter and I negotiated with the couple and finally agreed on a price. They wanted everything on the ranch included in the deal. I said, "No, I must have some things to work with. I'm going to keep the truck and a couple of horses."

They argued back and forth between themselves. At last we settled for the truck, most of our hand tools, a few pieces of furniture, and one saddle horse—my little bay mare, Betty.

After talking it over with Walter and Dad, we decided it would be best to keep just one horse. There were no fenced pastures on my homestead, so whatever hay we needed for the winter would have to be packed in over the mountain. There was no time to build a barn, and besides we had no lumber for it.

It was hard for me to accept the fact that we had to leave Las Lomas. On the other hand, I looked forward to my new adventure. I knew it would be rough the first year, especially since it was so close to winter.

Our ton-and-a-half truck was a 1929 Model A Ford, the first truck on which dual wheels could be installed. Walter and I had hauled at least 150 cords of wood with it. When we first started hauling heavy loads down those crooked mountain roads, the truck had big single tires on it. The twists and turns blew the back tires out every five thousand miles or less. We replaced them with smaller dual wheels. These dual tires had now gone sixty thousand miles and were still good.

Although it was a much bigger truck than I needed, I said to Walter, "We have it, it's paid for, so we're going to keep it." It was equipped with high stock racks and a ten-foot bed. We'd bought the truck new and had an extra Browning transmission installed. The gears could be shifted to compound every gear. That gave a range of twelve gears, counting overdrive. It could pull a load up the steepest mountain.

Many people had warned me: You can't possibly drive that truck over the old Smith Road. There was no time to waste arguing. We would have to move what I wanted over to the end of the road, then pack it in to the cabin site.

First Walter and I rode horseback over the divide and down into the cedars. We cut a bunch of cedar poles and built a corral. This gave me a place to store things.

The first thing I hauled over was a bunch of split lumber. The furniture, dishes and tools that I hauled over, I stacked in the corral and covered with a lot of old painted canvas. After several trips over to the corral, I met our neighbor Frank Fry. He had to back up a ways to let me by, so we stopped to talk.

Frank said, "By gosh, I saw those dual tire tracks, and I just had to stop and get out of my car and look to make sure my eyes weren't deceiving me. I couldn't believe you had driven down to your corral and made it out again."

"Some of the turns are a tight squeeze," I said, "One of the tires on the duals kind of runs on air for a short distance, but so far so good."

"We'll have to do a little more work on the road," Frank said.

The following winter Dad and I spent some time working on the road, using pick and shovel in the worst places. Much later I hauled cords and cords of wood over this road.

The great day came, on October 1, 1932, when Dad and I moved onto the homestead flat. We made a permanent camp close to where we planned to build the cabin. It was slow work to struggle up over the mountain with one horse, packing in all the material we needed from the corral, or pack station, as Dad and I called it. I did most of the packing, riding up and leading Betty back.

We had to cut more trees out of the trail to get the horse and pack through. I packed in boards and hand tools first. The boards were split, smooth sap boards Walter and I had made when we were working in the redwoods at Las Lomas. Walter had hewed a lot of ties and I split boards, shakes and posts, plus a lot of grape stakes.

After I packed the boards down to the camp, Walter came up from Santa Rosa and stayed with us for a week to help build the first room of the cabin. We decided on a site about forty feet back from the falls. Walter and I staked out a place fourteen by sixteen feet. "I'll take the mattock and shovel and level this off while you and Leona are getting logs," Dad said.

"That'd be a great help," Walter said.

"Walter, we don't want to get this cabin too big," I said. "The logs would be too hard to handle." I scratched a drawing in the dirt. "It has to be big enough to get in the heating stove, two single beds, a table and two chairs. I think we'd better make it twelve by fourteen."

"That's as good as anything," Walter said. "Let's go see what we can find in the way of logs."

The north side of the mountain going up from the flat was covered with trees, and we wandered through them. They didn't look good. Walter finally picked out a tree and chopped it down. I helped him trim off all the limbs. "Let's measure a sixteen foot length, just for fun," Walter said. It tapered down so fast it was out of the question to build a cabin of logs, even twelve feet long. We looked at one another and had a good laugh.

"Well, that's that," I said. "Why can't we make the cabin twelve by fourteen and find the four best logs we can for a foundation. Can you notch them at the corners, Walter? Then we'll lock them together for the foundation. Notch the big end of the log deep, and leave the little end as is. That will even it up. Think it would work?"

"Good idea. Let's try that."

"Another thing, why not use the split boards for the walls? They're so smooth we can nail them on up and down and later split a few of the boards into three-inch-wide strips for battens to nail over the joints or cracks. For the frame, or to take the place of the two by fours we don't have, we can use small round trees cut just short of six feet to hold up the top plate. We'll just have to find the best trees we can to make the top plate. Maybe you can trim the large end down some, to even up the plate. Let's cut these smaller trees a little less then six feet for studs. Leave the bark on, as it's so pretty with all its gray, brown, black and white color running through it."

"Let's put those in one every four feet. Should be close enough. The boards are almost three quarters of an inch thick. Leona, I think you've come up with a great idea."

We picked out four of the best trees and felled them. I helped him trim, then rolled them down to the flat Dad had graded off with the shovel and mattock. Walter told Dad what we had decided on. He thought it was a much better idea then trying to build a log cabin. Walter and I took a drink of the nice cold water and rested for a few minutes. The sun was up and shining on the flat.

"I can visualize a lot of good things on this flat when we get rid of some of the brush," Dad said.

Walter went to work on the logs. He cut them long enough to notch the corners. While he was notching, I gathered some flat rocks and we leveled the foundation logs with them. Walter and I hefted the logs and dropped them into place.

Dad stood there taking it all in. "Say, that looks good and it's going to stay there. There's no way it can go any place."

Walter and I climbed back up the mountain to look for the best small trees. We cut a bunch of them, trimmed them and carried them down to the cabin site.

"Let's put up our corner studs or poles first," Walter said. "We can level 'em if you happen to have any chalk line."

"Why can't we use the good old lariat?"

"Yeah, we can do that, and use the level on it. My, what would we do without those two things?"

We left the bark on the poles. We cut the so-called plates out of the smoothest trees we could find and spliced them in the middle so there wouldn't be so much taper. By being careful to cut each pole to its proper measure, we came out with a good, even wall.

Our lumber was only six feet long, so the wall and plate were not very high for the door. To compensate, we set the little porch floor six inches below the door jamb or floor level of the cabin. This way, when one walked out the door he would step down six inches and wouldn't bump his head.

By noon the next day we were ready to nail the boards on the walls. They went up fast, as we didn't bother with the battens until the walls were all on. We tied the walls across temporarily with three poles laid on top of the plates and nailed. These would be taken off after we had the rafters nailed in place. Now we cut poles for rafters.

By the third day we had the rafters up and nailed them together with a pole laid across them one foot above the plate. We pulled the three original poles off the top of the plate. Now we had head room if later I wanted to put in a ceiling. Walter and I trudged up the side hill and cut more poles to use as purlin to support the rafters the shakes would be nailed to.

In the south wall, I framed in a window six feet long and three feet high. The window had been brought over from the ranch, and I was fortunate to get it packed in without breaking it. It was in two sections. I placed them so one framed pane slid by the other one in a groove chopped and chiseled in the top edge of the windowsill log. I had this idea in my head, because the kitchen windows in the Las Lomas house were this way, only set in finished lumber.

Our project started coming to life and began to look like a real house, on a small scale.

The next day we finished nailing the purlin poles on.

"What are we going to do for shakes, Leona?" Walter asked.

I pondered a moment. "Do you think there'd be a chance of making shakes out of one of those big fir trees out on the mountain?"

"Great idea. Too bad we didn't have some left over at the ranch. We could have brought them. I don't know how fir shakes will work, but if they split good I don't see why they wouldn't be all right."

The next morning Walter saddled Betty and we loaded her with tools. Dad could ride; Walter and I walked out to the big timber. Walter picked out a medium sized fir, very smooth, a tall trunk, with no limbs for about forty feet. It was about two-and-a-half feet in diameter.

Dad took Betty's bridle off and led her down into some nice bunch grass. He let her drag her halter rope and she went right to eating. When Dad came back, Walter said to him, "This looks like a good tree. Do you want to pull the other end of the saw?"

"Sure, I'll pull. I want to see what kind of shakes a fir tree makes."

Dad helped Walter saw almost halfway through the tree about eighteen inches above the ground on the upper side. In order to get the tree to slip off the stump when it came down, Walter used his thin double-bitted ax to chop the underbit from the ground up. This is called sniping the stump. It allows the tree to slip down the face of the stump and lie flat on the slope of the mountain and prevents it from breaking or shattering when it hits the ground. On the back side of the tree, three inches above the undercut, Dad and Walter started a cut with the six-foot cross-cut saw. It didn't take long to saw through almost to the undercut.

"Better pull the saw out, and I'll drive a couple of wedges in the cut," Walter said. "That'll wedge it up the hill."

Dad did so and got back away from the tree. I was off to one side, watching the top. When Walter drove the wedges I could see the top of the tree quiver. It was leaning more and more up the hill.

"It's ready to go!" I hollered.

It hung there, so Walter chopped a few more chips out of the underbit.

I kept watching the top. "It's quivering! It's going-going!" I yelled. "Look out!"

Walter grabbed his ax and scrambled away. The tree leaned more and more, then came down with a boom and a huge cloud of dust. As the dust settled we walked over to the tree trunk.

"Looks like a pretty good log," Dad said.

"It does," Walter said, "but the only way to tell for sure is to get a cut out of it and see how well it splits."

Walter marked off a cut about thirty feet up from the butt end. "Come on, Dad," he said, picking up the saw.

The saw was sharp so it didn't take them long to saw through the log. Walter measured a three foot length, then they sawed through again. Dad pulled the saw out and laid it down. Walter picked up the Johnny Hale crowbar and pried the cut out to one side of the trunk.

The cut was checked or cracked across the center, so Walter placed his wedges in one crack and pounded them in with the sledge. It split with a pop, and each half lay out on the ground.

"Gee I think this is going to work. Hand me the checker, Leona."

He marked off a couple of eight inch shake bolts, then took the wedges and split them out. "Now comes the test," Walter said. He stood a bolt up on end against the end of the cut log, then placed the froe, or splitting tool, on top of the bolt, with the wood grain facing away from him. He pounded the froe down with a wooden mallet. It was splitting easily. As he pounded on the point of the froe that was stuck out on the side of the bolt, he pulled the end of the froe handle towards him to pry the shake off. By the time he had the froe two-thirds of the way down the bolt, the shake popped off.

"Hey, what do you think of that, Leona? Looks good. I split it a quarter of an inch thick, a little thick, but maybe I can make them thinner."

Shakes are split with the grain of the wood up, so there is a tiny trough for each drop of rain water to run down when the shake is nailed onto the roof. "I'll split up a few more bolts, then we'll have about a hundred shakes. We'll take 'em in and try nailing them on the roof."

As Walter split the shakes, I packed them back together the way they were split and wired each end with baling wire so they'd be easy to load onto the saddle horse. We made up four bundles of twenty-five shakes.

Dad and Walter loaded Betty with the shakes and we trudged back to the cabin, leaving the tools there. After lunch, we sawed one bunch in half at the center then laid the first row at the bottom of the roof, butted edge to edge and nailed. Now Walter took the full length shakes and laid them over the starter row, centering the shakes over the cracks. He nailed the bottom but the top was in a twist.

He said to me, "This shake has such a twist in it I can't get it down on the purlin to nail it." A purlin is a horizontal member supporting the rafters.

"I'll fix it," I said. "Wait'll I climb up on the roof." I scrambled up and stepped on the top corner of the shake. You can bet that brought it down. "Nail it, quick!"

Walter pounded the nails home. "What'll happen when you take your weight off?"

"Piffle, I don't know. It can't any more than split. Hold your breath as I release my weight."

Nothing happened, so Walter nailed on the rest, and I had to stand on the corners to get them down flat to nail. "Hurray, we're in business!" Walter said.

"Looks like they are going to work out fine," I said.

That evening after supper we made our work plans for the next day.

"Dad," Walter asked, "will you take Betty tomorrow and

pack the shakes in to the cabin while Leona and I make them?"

"Sure, Walter, it'll be a good job for Betty and me."

Next morning right after breakfast, Dad rode Betty, and Walter and I walked out to the shake tree. Walter started to split up the rest of the shake bolts. While he split them, I bundled the shakes up, twenty-five in a bundle, and tied bailing wire around each bunch, top and bottom. Walter and I split shakes until noon. Dad had already made two trips to the cabin, with loads of shakes. We loaded Betty once more, then we all walked back to the cabin for lunch. We had enough shakes for the time being, so we didn't go back out to the log any more that day. All the rest of the afternoon, Walter and I nailed on shakes.

By noon next day we figured we had enough shakes to finish the roof. After lunch, Walter and I were ready to nail more shakes.

The following day we were nearly done with the roof, and it looked good, too. Dad kept admiring the roof and giving us encouragement.

This was just the fourth day, and we were making good headway with the cabin. We still had the gable ends to fill in. We could either split some boards out of the fir or close it in with shakes. In the evening after supper I asked, "What are we going to do for a floor?"

Dad suggested we fill it in with dirt. I shook my head. "A dirt floor? That would be a true homestead floor, I guess, but I have a better idea. We'll do as Dad said, fill it in with dirt, but then we'll wheelbarrow some of the fine flat shale from the rocky ridge. I can make a wood tamper and tamp the fine shale into the dirt. Does that sound reasonable?"

"Should make a good floor," Walter said. "I think I'll go home tomorrow and see how my family is, but I'll come back next weekend, and Dean will probably come with me."

We had a big heavy wheelbarrow sitting up at the pack station. Dad said, "When you walk out tomorrow, we'll go up to the pack station with you and I'll bring the wheelbarrow in. Is that okay with you, Leona?"

"Sure Dad, the sooner we get it here the better. I'll make a tamper in the morning." We could get plenty of dirt along the back side of the cabin and top it off with fine shale pounded into the dirt. It was really getting chilly now in the evenings. Walter and I walked, while Dad rode Betty up to the car, and we told Walter goodbye.

I'll never forget the day of the wheelbarrow.

Dad said, "Leona, let's take the heating stove down to the cabin in the wheelbarrow."

"Dad! you can't possibly push that up over the mountain!"

"Well, if I can just get it to the top of the mountain, going down the other side will be easy."

"I have an idea. I'll tie the lariat to the wheelbarrow, then Betty can pull it by the saddle horn."

"By Jove, that'll work." We loaded the stove and I doubled the lariat, took the middle of it and made a slip knot around the front pipe frame of the wheelbarrow. I held onto the two ends of the rope, mounted up, took two wraps around the saddle horn and held it with my right hand.

You never tie the rope to the horn; this is called taking a dally around the horn. You hold onto the rope after you make the dally as a safety precaution. In case something happens, you can let go of the rope and it will be loose from the horse. "Are you ready, Dad?"

"Yes, let's see how this is going to work." The stove was loaded forward in the body of the wheelbarrow so there was not much weight on the handles. After we had gone a short way, Dad said, "This isn't bad at all."

Betty walked right along, pulling the wheelbarrow. We stopped and rested a few times going up the mountain so Dad could catch his breath. Going down the mountain was a snap. It didn't seem long before we were going over the rocky ridge. Dad had worked on this with the pick so the crossing was much better. We made it right up to the front of the cabin.

"That was a great way to get the stove down here," Dad said. "Betty did the hard work."

"Yes, it really worked out fine."

"We can haul dirt now," Dad said. Next morning we went up with the crosscut saw and cut a piece six inches thick and eight inches in diameter from one of the stumps. I took it down to the cabin, squared it up and drilled a hole in the center. Then I whittled a limb for a handle down to size with the hatchet, and drove it into the hole. The handle was about four feet long on my tamping tool. We started in after lunch. We didn't have to go very far for dirt as we got a lot when we smoothed the yard out around the cabin.

We filled in the front porch first. The dirt was dry, so we sprinkled several buckets of water on it so it would pack better. I tamped as Dad filled. I saddled Betty and had her pull the wheelbarrow loaded with shale rock. Dad held up the wheelbarrow handles. The rock was small, thin and flat. It looked like it would make a good floor.

The next morning we started on the room. I spread and tamped the dirt down as Dad wheeled it in and dumped it. It took many loads of dirt to fill it within two inches of the top of the foundation logs. Thank goodness we didn't have to haul the dirt very far. It took two days of hard work to fill, dampen and tamp the room. We didn't stint on rock, as we found out if it was tamped hard the floor was like a solid stone or slate floor. We had a good floor after five days of hard work. It would have been much more work to make it out of split lumber.

I had brought a ten-by-twelve-foot living room rug over from the ranch. First I had to pack it in on the horse. Friday morning I cut a twelve-foot square out of the painted canvas, laid it over the rock, then placed the rug on top of that. When we walked on it it felt like a padded carpet.

We installed the stove on hard packed shale rock on the north side. We left a space behind the stove and, by putting the ten-foot length of the carpet towards the stove, we left a strip of open rock around the stove.

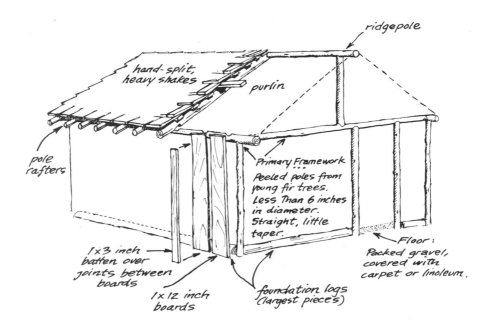

Construction of the cabin

The old heating stove had been in the family for years. It had the name Hazel across the front of it, just above the front doors which had isinglass across the top. When the fire was burning it was almost like sitting in front of a small fireplace. You could see the flames jumping around inside. There is something about watching flames and hot red coals in a fireplace that is very relaxing.

I had a good feeling in front of old Hazel. I can remember when I had an earache as a small child. My Mother held me on her lap right up close to this very same stove and the hot air made my earache go away.

Little did I know then that Hazel would be my friend for so many years. The stove had a flat top with two cookstove lids, good for cooking and heating water.

I built two wood-pole cot frames, one on each side of the stove with the heads against the north wall. I had cot springs and mattresses to go on these. I placed the six-foot pine table under the six-foot window on the south side of the room.

When anyone entered the cabin, invariably they would ask, "What kind of a floor do you have in here? It's so nice to walk on." Then I would have to tell the floor story.

At last we had things moved in. We had beaten the rain, but there was no door for the doorway. I hung a heavy blanket over it, which would have to do until I could get one built.

The first night in the cabin really felt good to us. By now the evenings were quite chilly as soon as the sun went down. That evening I cooked supper on the stove and we actually sat down to dinner where it was warm.

I had packed in the three-by-six foot table and two dining room chairs. With a carpet on the floor and a little imagination the cabin was as good as a castle.

Walter was due back the next evening. No doubt he would be pleased.

CHAPTER 6

WALLPAPER

The sun went down behind the little rocky ridge in a blaze of orange, yellow and red scattered over dark clouds, making me wonder what tomorrow might bring.

As I stepped out the door to call Dad to supper, I could feel the winter chill in the air. Old Hazel's fire kept the cabin warm. Dad was down feeding Betty her allotment of grain. He had brought her in from the side hill where she'd been grazing on green bunch grass. Betty liked her barley and would whinny for it.

Dad called back, "Be right there." After dinner dishes were done, we sat in front of the stove. The red hot coals and flames in old Hazel cast dark shimmering shadows on the gray board walls. An idea came into my mind.

"Dad, these walls would look much better if I covered them with wallpaper, something with bright autumn colors in it."

"Where are you going to get the paper?"

"I already have it. I saved all the rolls of left-over wallpaper from the time we did the living room over in Las Lomas."

"It would make the room much warmer too, Leona."

"First I'll need some heavy building paper to tack onto the boards, otherwise every crack will show through." Where there's a will, there's a way, I've always believed. "Dad, I know what I can do. Montgomery Ward in Santa Rosa always has lots of large cartons to give away. Why don't I go down and get a bunch of them?"

"Why don't you buy some rolls of building paper?" Dad asked. "Wouldn't they be easier to use?"

"Dad, I don't have any money. The mattress cartons will work fine. They're heavier than building paper, and I think the side of a carton would be just right to fill in between the small round stud poles."

Walter came back on the second Friday and I told him I'd go to Santa Rosa with him and bring the cardboard back in the truck.

Walter and I went hunting the next day. It was still cloudy and looked like it might rain any minute. We took turns walking and riding. Happy, my McNab shepherd dog, was with us. She liked to hunt wild hogs and that's what we hoped to find. There'd been no rain so it was hard to find any evidence of rooting; everything was so dry.

We circled around the top of fir mountain and saw only a few deer that trotted out ahead of us. Happy ran through the big manzanita patch on the south side of the mountain and found nothing. We decided it was just not our day.

Dad was cutting some stove wood on the flat when we came in. "Where are all those hogs you were going to get?" he asked.

"Oh, Leona and I left them for later," Walter said. "Maybe it will be better hunting next time I come up."

On Sunday, we all cleared manzanita in front of the cabin. Late that afternoon, Walter and I hiked over the mountain to his car at the pack station. We jumped in and Walter took off. It was fifty-two miles out to his house west of Santa Rosa.

Walter's wife, Maude, and Dean and his little sister, Doris, were glad to see me and I had a good visit with them that evening. Maude wanted to know everything I had done to the cabin, so we had plenty to talk about. Maude liked the wall paper idea.

The next morning I got in the truck. Walter said he would be back to the cabin in about three weeks unless he needed the truck for something. I drove to Montgomery Ward's store and asked about the cardboard.

"I bet I have just what you are looking for," the clerk said. "We just unpacked a load of mattresses this morning, so there are a lot of empty cartons out on the loading dock. You're welcome to as many as you want."

This was a streak of luck. Each side of the carton would cover one four-foot space between the upright stud posts, and the posts themselves, with their pretty bark covering, were already finished.

I quickly did some figuring in my head and came up with thirteen cartons, then decided I'd take a few extra. They wanted to get rid of them anyway. I threw them into the truck.

I suppose I could have bought a few rolls of building paper—it would be easier to pack on the horse—but this was the Great Depression. I didn't have money to spend on paper when I could get cardboard for nothing. Anyway the cardboard was heavier and would do a much better job. I climbed up over the rack and pulled the rope across the cardboard and tied it tight, so I didn't have to worry about losing any.

Maude's sister, Fern, owned a small grocery store on Benton Street in Santa Rosa, so I drove up there, visited a few minutes with her, then bought some groceries and put them in a wooden box in the cab of the truck. I made myself comfortable behind the steering wheel and took off for my 52-mile drive. I always enjoyed this drive, especially after I passed Skaggs Springs, for then it was all mountain driving. I saw deer, quail, and sometimes a rattlesnake along the bank.

I felt pretty good until I thought about how I was going to get the cardboard into the cabin without getting any creases in it. A good question.

After I passed Las Lomas, the next ten miles were slow miles, but I didn't mind. I turned off onto the old sled road for much slower driving. When I drove by the old orchard, deer ran in every direction. I stopped to watch them, then a funny thing happened. An old doe was watching me as she walked away, and she walked right into a stump and was upended over it. I laughed; it's so seldom one sees deer do anything clumsy. She got up on her feet, then took off in a hurry.

I continued on my way and soon reached the pack station. I left the groceries in the cab of the truck and walked into the cabin. Dad was glad to see me, and the first thing he asked was, "How'd you make out with the cardboard?"

"Oh, land sakes, I picked up enough cardboard to do all the walls and have plenty left over."

The next morning Dad saddled Betty for me and I rode up to the truck. I carefully took the cartons apart, then rolled three at a time into a big round cylinder and tied them with baling wire. I tied a roll on each side of the saddle, and one on top and I put the groceries in a grain sack in the saddle before I loaded the top roll. Going up the trail, Betty looked like something from a foreign planet, or like a bunch of big hollow culverts weaving and wobbling up the mountain through the trees.

The next day I cut cardboard to fit between the upright poles with the pretty bark on them and tacked it tight to the boards. It took me most of the day, so I didn't try any wall paper.

Dad had worked in the flat for a while. He couldn't work too long as he had a bad hernia. Lifting really bothered him. I think that is one reason he liked to saw wood. I'd see him sitting down a lot and just pulling that saw back and forth, maybe humming a little tune. He didn't enjoy hunting and horseback riding.

That evening, in front of the stove, I said, "I'm going to paste the paper on the walls tomorrow."

"Think you can do it in one day?"

"Oh, I think so, it's such a low wall."

Most ranchers used old kerosene lamps at night. We were fortunate to have a couple of Aladdin lamps. We'd used them for years at Las Lomas, and I'd brought them with me. They had a mantle over a round wick, and a tall chimney helped them burn evenly. They burned kerosene and gave a white light, about equal to a 75-watt light bulb. It was surprising how long a mantle lasted if a person was careful to not jar the lamp.

Dad and I liked to sit and visit in the evening by firelight. Dad had many interesting stories to tell about his life's work. One he liked to tell was of the time he and his brother, William, plowed and sowed the 640 acre wheat ranch over in Elk Grove. He said, "Will and I used to plow a quarter of a section, forty acres at one time. After plowing, Will hitched eight horses to a sixteen-foot harrow and I did the same. We drove over the plowed ground with the harrows to break up the clods.

"After the ground was ready to sow, I took his team and harrow and hitched them alongside my team, chaining the harrows together. I then had a sixteen-horse hitch and a thirty-two foot harrow. Will had the seeder wagon with another four horse team hitched to it. He drove over the harrowed field and seeded it. I drove the big team and harrow behind him to cover the seeded ground. It took some doing to know when to start turning this big team around at the end of the field. That's why I've always spaded the gardens by hand: there just isn't room to turn even one horse and a plow around without packing the ground all down."

That night Dad told me he and Will kept thirty-five to forty horses, and in wintertime they were turned out in a forty-acre field. In the fall, after the wheat had been thrashed, he and his brother raked up the straw and stacked it.

I can remember going to this ranch for visits with Uncle Will and Aunt Julia, my mother's sister, and playing hide-and-seek with their children in and around these big hay stacks. They had three boys and five girls. The horses had eaten huge holes into the stacks of straw, so it made a great place for this kind of a game.

The next morning I went right to work on the wall-papering. I worked until noon, then fixed lunch, and went back to papering. Dad came in as I was finishing up late that afternoon. "My land, Leona, that surely looks nice. Funny how some cardboard, paper and paste can make such a difference in a room. That just looks great."

"Yes, Dad, but I'm not finished. I have curtains to put up over the dining room window and tie back."

I made a curtain rod of a very small tree that I trimmed down to a pole the width of the window. I sawed out two blocks of wood with grooves in the tops to hold the rod. I nailed these blocks at the top of the window. I ran the pole through the top hem of the curtain, then placed the rod on the two blocks. My curtains were hung—and I pushed each one back to the side so we could see out. The room looked cozy and warm now. I did need a front door, though, in place of the blanket.

"Guess my next job is to build a door," I said.

"Yes, it'd be nice to get one up before rain," Dad said.

It's a shame so many people say they would never have a fireplace or a wood stove: "Too much wood to carry in and ashes to carry out." True, but they don't realize the enjoyment, the difference in the warmth of the room. Besides, bringing the wood in is wonderful exercise, or a good chore for one of the children. Ashes spread over the garden grow big vegetables to make everybody strong and healthy.

Old Hazel did everything that first winter. All the meals were cooked on her lid. I even baked delicious bread on the top by putting the loaves in a pan set on a wire rack, then a pan over the bread pan, tight down on the top of the stove. (I was glad it had a flat top.) I baked beans that way, and heated all my wash water and, when it rained, I hung clothes to dry by the heat of old Hazel.

One of Dad's hobbies was to keep track of every drop of rain. My stars and little fishes, did it ever rain! By the time spring came, Dad had measured 108 inches, compared to our annual average of 16 inches. Fortunately there were plenty of places for it to run down the canyon. Dad recorded the rainfall every year in his diaries.

Dad loved to cut wood, so I always had plenty of dry wood. On many ranches, the men got as far as the chopping block and there they seemed to bog down. A lady who lived down the creek about fifteen miles always had to go out and chop kindling and stove lengths off the limbs to get a fire to cook with.

My parents were different, though. Firewood is the only thing I can remember Mother and Dad disagreeing about when I was a child at Las Lomas. Dad kept a long row of stovewood ricked up against a picket fence, so when he walked up from the barn he would pick up an armload of wood to carry to the big woodbox by the stove. But he didn't stop there. He filled the firebox of the stove, never thinking of what Mother might be baking. Well, quite often the bread had a very dark complexion, or the crust had been trimmed off because it had been burned. Mother would say, "Dad, you stuffed the stove again!"

"Yes, I can see by the bread. I'll try to do better next time. I should look in the oven."

But there were lots of times the bread had its shiny deep brown coloring, because he stuffed the firebox. Another habit was when he would come in the house and, thinking Mother was going to let the tea kettle run dry, fill it up with cold water. Well, Mother probably was waiting for a little hot water. To top it off, invariably he would say on wash day, "Gee, don't we get apple pie today?" As if she hadn't enough to do, with all the washing.

Truly, I never heard them argue or raise their voices to one another. As I said, Winona and I had a great childhood. I think that's one reason I've always loved ranch life and the outdoors. I look forward to each day's adventure. It might only be a new wildflower to look up in the book, but there's always something different.

CHAPTER 7

WILD GOATS

Our first year at the cabin, Walter and Dean spent a few days with us during Christmas vacation. It was raining hard.

"My gosh, Aunt Nono, do you think it's ever going to stop?"

"Yes, Dean, there's always a silver lining to a cloud. The sun will shine when the great father in heaven wills it to."

The third day the sun came out strong. Dean could hardly wait to go hunting. He ran out in the yard where his Dad and Granddad were cleaning out a ditch. "Dad, is it all right if I take my rifle and go out onto the mountain for a little while?"

"Yes, if you're careful. Don't stay out too long."

"Gosh, Dad, you know me, I'll be careful. Shall I shoot a hog if I see one?"

"Yes, by all means, we can use the meat. You know what to do first thing if you do shoot one?"

"Yes, Dad, I bleed it, then come back to get you."

"Okay, you can go."

Dean rushed back into the cabin. "Aunt Nono, I'm going out on Fir Mountain. Maybe I can find a hog."

"Remember, Dean, you have a rifle in your hands, so be careful."

"Yes, Aunt Nono." He picked up his rifle, dashed out the door and we could hear him whistling as he hurried down the flat.

It had rained so hard that mud washed up against the

back wall of the cabin, so Walter and Dad were digging a bigger ditch for drainage and I was cleaning away tracked-in mud. Everybody was so busy it didn't seem any time until Dean was back. I heard him talking to his Dad, and by the tone of his voice was excited. I went to the door to listen.

"Dad! Do you know what I got?"

"I bet you killed a wild hog."

"Oh no, Dad, I shot two big billy goats. They have great big curled horns."

"Billy goats?"

"Yeah, you oughta see 'em."

"Dean! what in the world are you going to do with them?"

"Gee, I don't know. Nothing I guess." The excitement over his hunt was leaving fast.

His Dad looked at him for a minute. "Dean, you can't go out and kill something that can't be used and let it lie there just because you wanted to shoot your rifle."

"Gee, Dad, what do I do now? They stink so bad I can't get close to them."

Walter waited a few seconds before answering. "After you have your lunch, I think the best thing you can do is take your hunting knife, go back out there and skin both animals."

"Oh gee! Dad, do I have to do that? They smell terrible."

"Yes, you can't go hunting and shoot animals and just let them lay. That is an absolute rule in hunting."

"Well, it's going to be an awful smelly job."

His Dad looked at him with a slight smile. "Dean, you're the one who created this situation, so you'd better enjoy the spoils of hunting. Just think! It may never happen again!"

I went back inside the cabin and prepared lunch, then called them in to eat. Dean never said a word.

After we finished lunch, Dean reluctantly picked up his rifle and left for his disgusting task. This time he wasn't whistling as he ambled down the flat. The men went back to their yard work. It was well over three hours before we saw Dean again. As soon as he crossed the little rocky ridge and came down into the flat, we all got a whiff of the sickening, foul odor of the billy goats. He walked up to the cabin and threw a hide down.

His Dad greeted him. "My Lord, son, take that hide back over the ridge and hang it on a limb somewhere. We can't have that stink by the cabin. Did you skin both of 'em."

"Yeah, but the skins were so heavy I could only carry one."

He took the hide away, but when he came back he smelled as bad as the goat.

Walter rushed into the cabin, "Leona, will you stir up the fire while I go get some water from the creek? Dean stinks so of those blasted billy goats, he's got to take a bath."

When the water was warm enough I brought the washtub in and poured. Walter went to get more water so I could wash Dean's clothes later, then he called Dean to come in and take his bath. I think he used about half a bar of Fels-Naphtha soap, trying to get rid of that horrible odor. I used the other half scrubbing his clothes. I really don't know who suffered the most from that hunt: Dean, his granddad or me. Every time it rained, even long after, the moisture brought out that sickening billy goat aroma.

Dean promised me, "I'll never shoot another billy goat as long as I live."

CHAPTER 8

HUNTERS' STORY

In March of 1933 we had a heavy rainstorm. The morning after the storm was clear and cold. The sky was a bright blue; the day promised to be beautiful and all the trees glistened from the rain and the reflection of the sun on the leaves.

"You know," I said to Dad, "This would be a great day to find a wild hog."

"Golly, it would be fine if you could get one. The ones we've had have been such good meat."

I saddled Betty, who was tied to a tree, and led her back to the cabin and threw her reins down. Then I picked up my rifle and some extra shells, went out and mounted up.

"I'll probably be gone a couple of hours at least, Dad. I'm going out on Fir Mountain."

"Don't be gone too long. If you get a big one, come back and get me. I'll help you load it."

Happy, my McNab shepherd dog, was eager to go. She was rather a small dog with short thick black hair, white markings on her neck and big brown eyes that almost talked. Her long tail wagged hard when she was happy, which was most of the time. She was always glad to see me saddle up, because she liked to tag along.

"Bye, Dad," I said, and rode out across the flat through manzanita. Every bush looked like it had been scrubbed, the leaves were so clean from the heavy rain. I rode into the fir timber on top of the mountain. It was damp with deep shade,

Blacktail deer

and where it opened on the west side I found a huge grassy area that sloped almost down to Cedar Creek.

On my left rose a large patch of manzanita, warm because the bright sun shone directly on it from the south. I soon found signs of hog rooting in the damp earth. Happy picked up the scent and took off, running first this way, then that, following the scent. I jumped off my horse, pulled the reins over her head and threw them down on the ground. Then I heard Happy barking. I knew by the sound of her voice she was baying something, running around and around, holding it in one place.

I jerked my rifle out of the scabbard, levered a cartridge into the chamber and eased the hammer down on half cock so it would be safe. Leaving Betty standing there, I ran towards Happy's barking. In some places the brush was so thick and stiff I had to drop to my knees and crawl under it. Before long I was close enough to see where Happy had a nice hog bayed.

With Happy running circles around the hog, it was hard to get a shot. The hog was turning as fast as the dog. Finally Happy stopped and looked at me as much as to say, "Holy Smoke, why don't you shoot this thing?" That was the chance I'd been waiting for. I raised my rifle and shot for the ear. The hog never knew what hit him. Happy ran to me. I petted her and told her what a good dog she was. She looked up at me with those big brown eyes, her tail going a mile a minute in a big circle to tell me it was all so much fun!

I took my pocket knife and bled the hog, then field-dressed it. Now came the real work. I made my way back to Betty, shoved my rifle in the scabbard and picked up her reins. We started off, twisting and turning here and there to work through the brush, back to the hog.

Betty always had an act to go through before I could put a deer or hog on her. I don't know why; maybe it was the smell of the blood. She jumped and snorted around until I could shove her up against some heavy brush before she would stand still.

I struggled to lift the hog high enough to get it into the saddle so it would balance when I tied it down. The hog probably weighed close to a hundred pounds. If you have never lifted a limp hog shoulder high, I suggest you try it some time.

At last I had it loaded and tied to the cinch ring so it couldn't move while the horse was moving. I picked up the reins. "Come on Betty, let's go home."

Some hunters would have loaded it behind the saddle and ridden home. I always thought that was asking too much of the horse, and besides, it could get warm from the body heat of the horse.

I enjoyed the chance to walk while Betty carried the load. Happy was still interested in the hog and every once in a while glanced up at it. Dad was in the cabin when I arrived, and I hollered, "You'd better come out and see what we brought!"

Dad rushed out and his eyes popped. "By Jove! you did it, didn't you? Say, that looks like a dandy. You must have had a time getting it loaded."

"Did I! I thought for a while I was going to have to get you out to the rescue. I finally made it." I led Betty to a tree to tie her up, and Dad helped me hang up the hog. "I'll skin it in the morning," I said. "It'll be nice and cold then, the hide will come off easier, and the meat will be smooth and pebbly."

To explain this, you may know that tame hogs, after they are killed, are scalded in a barrel of hot water. Then the hair is taken off with scrapers. Wild hogs are hung by the head overnight to cool. In the morning, you take your pocket knife, wrap adhesive tape around the blade to about an eighth- to one-quarter inch from the point, depending on the thickness of the hide, and proceed to cut strips about two-and-one-half to three inches wide from the nose down to the hind feet. You get this started with the pocket knife and take hold of the strip with a pair of pliers and pull it right off the hog. When it's all off, it leaves a pebble effect on the hog. It's a neat way to get the hide off.

We usually let them hang for three or four days. If there were any flies in the area, we covered the meat with flour sacks, but removed them at night so the cold air could blow on the meat.

You may wonder what kept the saddle horse standing when the reins were thrown to the ground. They're trained to this when very small, or when broken to ride. This is called ground tied. We had broken Betty as a colt.

First the colt is broken to a halter, then tied to a root, a log or even a rock. At first, they're left long enough so they don't fight it. Then they're left maybe all day in one spot. They can turn around but there is nothing for them to tangle in and they can't go anywhere. When Dad and I broke Betty, we left her tied all day and all night.

I guess the horse, after being broken to ground tying, never realizes it can walk off. Some horses learn to feed by backing up so they don't step through the loop of the reins. I have had horses that stood all night and half the next day. In fact Betty did that.

One time at the old ranch, Dad packed some hunters out to a camp, and it was dark before he arrived home. He was riding one horse and leading Betty and another one. Well, he dropped Betty's rope and didn't miss it for a while. He did go back a ways to look for her, but he couldn't find her in the dark, so he turned around and went to the house.

The next day, right after lunch, he went out to look for her and she was standing right where her rope had dropped to the ground. Now, that's a well-trained horse.

CHAPTER 9

FLAMES AND A MOUSE TRAP

Although caught in the horrible Great Depression, I was enjoying myself and the cabin. I'd worked hard on the Las Lomas Ranch, helping my father and brother in the woods. We made a great many redwood railroad ties, posts, grape stakes, split boards and shakes.

These items had to be dragged or packed by horses out of the woods to a small flat and stacked. Years before, a sled road had been graded down into this canyon to the flat. Dad, Walter and I worked on it with hand tools until you could drive a small truck over it. We had a one-ton model T Ford truck, and it was usually my job to load the truck with the split material on the flat, haul it to the top of the ridge and stack it. The split three-, four- and five-foot grape stakes were stacked by the thousands. Railroad ties were stacked by size, the small ones (6 by 8 inches by 8 feet) in one stack and the large ones (8 by 10 inches by 8 feet) in another stack. The butt cut large ties frequently weighed 125 pounds each.

In 1924, my brother hired Ivan Hickman, who lived in Healdsburg and owned a two-ton hard tire Republic truck, to haul these products to Geyserville where Mr. Hickman unloaded and stacked them on the railroad siding. Later, Walter and a couple of hired men loaded them onto freight cars and shipped them to their destination.

We also had sheep to take care of. They had to be rounded

up at least four times a year. There was shearing, marking of
the lambs, tagging, and a round-up to pull out the lambs to go
to market. We built redwood picket corrals under some big
oak trees up on a knoll, located so that it saved herding the
sheep a mile and a half into the corrals at the barn when it
came time to round them up. A few of the sheep might need
tagging, or we might want to pull out some lambs for market.

In years gone by, school was held under one of these large
oaks for the neighborhood children, so these corrals were
always known as the Schoolhouse Tree corrals, or the Dixon
corrals.

Many times I took Jack, an older dog, and Happy, who
was not much more than a puppy learning the business, and
rode the lower south side trail and hollered the sheep up to
the top of the ridge. They would drift out to the line fence. By
the time I rode around the trail they would be scattered out
along this fence, and Jack, Happy and I could gather them in
a band and drive them back to the corrals.

Now at the cabin I was resting, hunting, fishing, riding
horseback to explore the country, and building when I felt
like it. I also had time to enjoy some reading. I did not have
Jack; he was now Walter's dog.

It is true that I didn't have any money to speak of, but that
didn't bother me a bit. Dad seemed quite happy. He had no
bad habits: he didn't smoke, chew tobacco, or drink, so he had
very little to buy. When he did get a little money, he usually
bought some carpenter's tool for me to use.

Other people, especially in the big cities, could not cope
with life in the Depression. They could see no future. Lots of
people lost all their money and property and had no place to
go and took their own lives.

I had a wonderful sister-in-law, Walter's wife, Maude,
and a terrific friend in her sister, Fern. Fern and her husband,
Guy, owned a small but successful grocery store in Santa
Rosa. I know now, looking back on it, that she sent groceries
that she never charged us for. Of course, I always took them a
roast of pork or meat of some kind. I guess these are the

returns the Bible means by "You shall reap what you shall sow."

Their two daughters, both grandmothers now, still talk of the good times they had when they came up to the homestead with their Uncle Dick (Walter).

When the children were little they couldn't pronounce Leona, so they called me Nono. When grandnieces and nephews came along, some called me Lono, I guess because I didn't marry until I was 69 years old (to a wonderful man named John).

During the winter, I built shelves across the corner opposite the foot of my bed, for writing paper and magazines. On the middle shelf I kept a big bowl of kitchen matches.

Once, I woke up in the middle of the night to find flames shooting up from the middle shelf! I flew out of bed, rushed to the water bucket and began throwing dipperful after dipperful of water on the fire. I finally doused the flames. It was a good thing, because I was out of water. "Oh, well," I told myself, "another day another adventure." Adventure could come in the middle of the night.

Dad didn't even wake up. I had to tell him all about it the next morning. "What do you suppose started the fire, Leona?"

"I imagine a pesky little mouse chewed one of those matches I had in the bowl, and that set them all off. They made some nice red flames for a few minutes."

"Good thing you woke up when you did; we could have lost the whole cabin."

"The cabin isn't much, but it would be a tremendous loss to us right now. Gee, I bet that little mouse took off in high gear when that match flamed up. Wonder if he singed his whiskers."

We laughed about it, but Dad said, "You'd better put the matches in a can after this."

"Yes, but we don't have any matches now, so you'd better keep that fire going. Walter doesn't smoke so he won't have any matches with him when he comes up."

"Gee, that's right. It's a good thing there were some coals in the stove when I got up this morning to make a fire."

That experience taught me a lesson. Henceforth the matches were always kept in an empty coffee can with the lid on tight. In those days it was a tin lid.

I was without a mouse trap, a simple thing when a person can run down to the corner store and buy some, but we were thirty miles from a store of any kind.

I decided I surely could outthink a tiny mouse. I took a tin feed bucket and made a wooden top for it. I cut a little hole in the center of the top and fashioned a trap door about three inches long and two inches wide with a small butt hinge cut out of a piece of thin tin with a small nail for the pivot. I tacked the butt end of the hinge to the top with the little door over the hole. It swiveled on the nail that held them together. I crimped a lip on the back door and the front of the hinge to hold the nail, then built a tiny box just past the door, with a hole in the front facing the trap door that he was to walk onto to get the jelly I would bait the trap with.

The next night I filled the bucket half full of water and set it on the floor over by the table, then baited the little box. That night, when Mr. Mouse went after the jelly, he tiptoed onto the little trap door, which was held in place by a strip of paper. When the mouse stepped upon the door, oops! The paper gave way and little mouse went slipping and sliding down the door like a swimmer going down the slide into a swimming pool. "I'm sorry little mouse but I can't have you running all over my house setting it on fire."

The mouse trap worked so well I caught a good many more little furry creatures that winter. I guess they thought the cabin was a cozy winter hideaway.

CHAPTER 10

THE START OF A GARDEN

Spring was on its way. The frost had finally decided to look farther north. Little green shoots of grass and a few small wild flowers were popping up out of earth warmed by the ever- increasing heat of the sun. Evenings were still cool enough to have a fire. We'd been without matches for some time, and Dad had kept the fire burning or kept the coals covered with ashes through all this time. When Walter came back the second time, we again had matches.

Walter had been up in January and again in early February. I always gave him a list of groceries to bring back when he made his monthly trip. March, however, was almost gone and he hadn't come up.

"We're out of groceries, Dad," I said. "All we have is what's left of the small hog I killed two weeks ago."

"I thought sure Walter would be back before now," Dad said. "How long has it been?"

"Five weeks. Wonder if there's something wrong? I could ride down to Effie and Lea Nobles and get some groceries from them, I'm sure, but my goodness, by the time I returned it would be a sixty mile ride. Or, I could go up to Frank Fry's. If he had any to spare he'd let us have some, but it's doubtful he's at his cabin. The new people on Las Lomas ranch aren't friendly, so I hate to ask them for anything."

"Surely, Leona, Walter will be here by Friday evening."

"I'll wait until Saturday noon. In the meantime, I'll grind up what dried corn we have, maybe make some hotcakes, but

I don't imagine they'll taste like much without baking powder."

The rest of the week we ate fried meat and a couple of meals of hotcakes with no baking powder or milk in them. I can't say I'd care for that as a steady diet. Friday night went by and nobody came. Saturday morning we had a slice or two of meat, lunch the same. That was it. One o'clock I walked down to Betty and was about to saddle her when someone hollered. Walter and Dean were coming across the little rocky ridge. I ran over to the trail to meet them.

The first thing Walter asked was, "Are you and Dad all right?"

"Yes, but we're getting extremely tired of meat."

"I was afraid of that."

We continued to the cabin and when Walter walked in, Dad's eyes got as big as saucers.

He said, "By golly, am I glad to see you! I hope you've brought a few groceries. Leona's cooking has gotten terribly monotonous lately."

"Yes, Dad. Dean and I packed some in with us and I'll take the horse and go back for the rest."

I said, "First, let me make some coffee. What else do you have?"

"How about a can of baked beans and some bread and butter for lunch? We can have potatoes and other things for supper when I get back with the rest."

"Sounds good to me."

I put lunch on the table and Walter said, "We all had the flu, is why I didn't get up two weeks ago. I've been worried about you running out of groceries."

"We've just about finished up all the meat. We're completely out of everything else."

"Dean wants to go hunting," Walter said. "How do you feel about going out?"

"Yes. Maybe Happy could find a pig or two for us while you go up to the pack station."

It worked out very well. Walter brought the groceries in,

and Dean, Happy and I went out into the fir and tanoak timber on the mountain and Happy bayed some nice hogs. Dean and I each got one. We dressed them out, and I told Dean we would get them in the morning.

Next morning, Dean, Walter and I loaded the two hogs on Betty and brought them in. We hung them and skinned them. Walter would have a nice hog to take home with him. They were in fine shape to make good meat. I guess they weighed about 125 pounds apiece. We had meat again, but I was glad to have the groceries to go with it.

We sat around the fire listening to KSL radio out of Salt Lake City. Dad and I liked to hear the Ames Brothers harmonize. The radio, an old Atwater-Kent, had been given to Dad by one of his deer hunting friends, Mr. West from Santa Rosa. We really enjoyed it. Being able to get the evening news made us feel less isolated. It used large drycell batteries. We used the radio about an hour in the evening, then shut it off to save the batteries.

One day, Dad asked, "Leona, do you think we could grow vegetables here on the flat?"

"I don't see why they wouldn't do well. The grass is beginning to come. Where would you put a garden?"

"There's a nice place halfway down the flat, on the upper side of the trail. It's nearly level and the sun shines on it almost all day this early in the spring."

"I've looked at that spot, too, with the same thought in mind, but there's a lot of brush in there."

"It's mostly small manzanita, not hard to get out."

"If you want to make the patch into a vegetable garden, I'll help you. We can shovel manure from down where Betty is tied and wheel it over there. That would be good to work into the soil. A nice vegetable garden would add variety to our meals this summer."

"It's early, and besides, Leona, we can't plant until Walter gets back here a second time."

We worked the following week on the garden area, cutting brush. Dad sawed up what was big enough for wood, and I collected the small dry brittle manzanita limbs for kindling. A lot of brush had died so it was easy to get the stumps out.

Manzanita stump makes a wonderful fire; it burns down to a very hot coal. In fact, the old mountaineers used it in their hand forges to heat and shape horseshoes. An old pitch fork with a broken handle didn't lie around long. It was heated, probably with the manzanita wood burned to hot coals, and pounded out on the anvil in the shape of a gig to catch steelhead with.

Nearly all the ranchers had a gig hidden in some tree near the creek. If he happened to ride by and saw that the steelhead were up, he picked up his gig and followed the creek a ways and gigged one to take home for fish dinner. With cream gravy, what could be better?

At Las Lomas, Dad had always had a beautiful big vegetable garden. He also planted a quarter acre of potatoes. Those plants grew enough potatoes to nearly last us a year. In the spring of every year, when Dad and I were cleaning up the yard around the house, he would say to me, "I can't see putting much time in on flowers, you can't eat 'em."

He left the yard planting to Mother and me. We planted many marigolds and among our beds of bulbs were tiger lilies, fawn lilies and a few brown lilies. We hung flower baskets all along the porch.

Winona liked to sew, knit, crochet and tat. Mother taught her these things. Winona liked horseback riding but never cared for hunting, although she was an excellent pistol shot. She could stand on the porch and shoot the clothespins off the line thirty- five feet away, one right after another, bang, bang, bang!

Mother was a talented person. Before we twins were born, she'd won a scholarship in pen and ink drawing. Mother hand-painted china and did some lovely wildflower paintings in oil and watercolor, as well as beautiful pen and ink illustrations. Believe it or not, she was a good carpenter as well as a writer of poetry and jingles. Mother and I were always building something. That's where I learned so much that was useful to me later.

I did miss the music at the homestead. Winona and I had made enough money running a trap line to buy a piano, but now it was gone with the ranch. Mother knew enough music to start us out, and we played piano, ukulele and mandolin. I later learned the 120 bass accordion.

For years we were plagued by bad luck. In March of 1924 we lost the Las Lomas house to fire. We lost everything. Because of the fire we lost the ranch, since Walter and I couldn't work in the woods that year, work which brought in a considerable amount of cash. We built a new house instead, but there was little insurance money, nothing on the contents. When the Depression hit, income from stock fell to nothing.

Oh, well, such is life. One has to take the good with the bad. As I always told myself, "Never, never give up."

I still desired to own a big stock ranch some day. I believed that market conditions would change. I didn't know what I would do to earn money, but I sure didn't want to be shut up in an office all day. I had worked in an office the year after I graduated from high school. I didn't exactly dislike the job; it was just being closed in so tight. No hills, no animals to love and no sky to look at all day long.

"Time will tell," I told myself.

CHAPTER 11

ADVENTURE MOUNTAIN

We called the fir-covered mountain Fir Mountain, but at times I thought I ought to rename it Adventure Mountain. Everything seemed to happen or finish on that mountain. The following episode happened the first year on our homestead.

The fall had been rainy, but this morning it was clear and the rays of the sun were peeking over the top of the mountain east of the cabin. I saddled Betty, led her up to the cabin and threw her reins down. Dad was out in the yard. "I'm going to ride out onto the mountain," I said.

"Don't stay out too long," he said, "and remember, if you need help to load a big hog, come back for me and I'll give you a hand."

"All right, Dad. Don't expect me back for two or three hours."

I gathered the reins, took hold of the saddlehorn, and swung up into the saddle. My rifle was in the scabbard. Happy was jumping up and down, glad to know we were going somewhere. I rode out on the trail and turned left where it forked to the pack station, riding through scrubby manzanita and loose rock. Nature had taken care of its housework. All the rocks had shining faces from so much rain. As I started to climb Fir Mountain, I rode into heavy fir timber and decided to ride around the north side of the mountain.

I had never been in there before. There were a lot of pepperwood, a deep green-leafed evergreen tree with a pungent spicy aroma. If you labored in it all day, cutting limbs and working in the leaves, it gave you a severe headache. The tanoaks, an evergreen that produced an acorn which made good hog feed in the fall of the year when they were ripe, were also thick. The pepperwoods had a nut that dropped in the fall, too, so the combination made a great place for hogs.

I soon came upon fresh hog rooting. Happy picked up the scent right away and took off tracking, her nose right down on the ground. I stopped and sat still on my horse, waiting to hear Happy bark. It wasn't long until I heard her. I listened a minute or two to determine if she was staying in one place.

She was. I could tell by her slow even bark that she had the hog, or hogs, bayed up in a circle. She was no doubt holding them by running around them while waiting for me to come to the rescue. I took off on Betty as fast as she could go. I got fairly close, jumped off, threw the reins down, pulled my rifle out of the scabbard, pumped a cartridge into the chamber and let the hammer down on half cock.

Happy had something bayed in a bunch of thick pepper-woods. The trees had been broken down by heavy snow at one time but were still very much alive. The heavy foliage prevented me from seeing the pigs. I kept circling the mass of deep foliage and finally glimpsed a hog. Happy stopped to look at me, which gave me a chance for a shot. One shot to the ear is all it took. The hog dropped right there.

After all the excitement, I had to answer nature's call. I walked around the mountain a little ways and proceeded to pull my Levis down. I backed up against a big fir tree. I had reloaded my rifle and stood it up against the tree alongside of me. All I lacked to be comfortable was a Monkey Ward Catalog.

Oh my! Oh my! Happy was barking excitedly and coming my way! I had just enough time to grab my rifle and pull the hammer back. The hog was almost upon me! He came so close so fast I barely had room to point the rifle without hitting the pig with the end of the barrel. I pulled the trigger as it passed me, and the hog and dog went out of sight.

I got my Levis in order, grabbed my gun and ran around the mountain to where Happy was jumping up and down and back and forth, barking. She was right on the edge of a steep drop-off into a narrow ravine. I looked down over the edge but couldn't see a thing.

"What in the world is the matter with you, Happy? You gone nutty? I can't see anything."

She stopped, looked at me in a funny way as if to say, "I think you're so dumb! Don't you believe me?" She ran down the hill a short ways, jumped down into the ravine and came back almost under me. She started pulling and tugging on something, and sure enough she had a hog in there. She had pushed so much dirt and leaves off the bank the hog was almost buried.

I walked down to the place where Happy had jumped into the ravine, sat down, slid to the bottom and walked back up to the hog. Happy's tail was going in circles. She looked at the hog, then at me. I reached down and petted her. "Oh, Happy, you're the greatest dog! That is just fine! You're such a good dog, you never fail."

She looked up at me with those big brown eyes and her tail wagged as if to say, "I did my best." After I petted her, we went back to the first pig. It was much smaller. I dragged it out from under the pepperwoods and field-dressed it. I guessed its weight after dressing to be eighty-five pounds, a nice size to make wonderful meat for eating.

"Let's take Betty to get the other hog," I said to Happy, picking up the reins and leading the horse over to the edge of the ravine. I slid down into the ravine again and walked back up to the hog. I dug the leaves and dirt away from it with my hands. With a lot of strong pulling, I managed to get it out from under the bank to give me room to dress it out. I began to wonder how in the world I was going to get it out of there. I remembered Dad saying, "If you get a big one, come back and get me."

"Gee," I thought, "that'll take a lot of time and mean a lot of walking for both of us. There must be another way." I thought for a few minutes and decided that Betty could pull it out.

I never went anywhere without my rifle and rope. I led Betty over to the bank where I had slid into the ravine, threw her reins down, took the lariat and walked back to the hog. I put two half hitches around both hind feet above the ankle joints. I took the other end of the lariat out to Betty, climbed into the saddle and took two dallies around the saddle horn. I raised the reins a little on Betty's neck and gave her a little kick with my heel. She walked down the hill and as she felt the rope tighten she leaned into the pull. In nothing flat the hog was up on the bank. Happy ran alongside, taking nips at it. I guess she thought it had come to life again. Now, this was a big hog! How in the world was I ever going to get it up into the saddle? I guessed its weight at over two hundred pounds.

I saw a big tanoak tree nearby. It had a thick limb growing out almost horizontal from the trunk, up about eight feet. I thought I could use it. I had Betty drag the hog over close to the tree, then I threw the end of my lariat over the limb. I took another rope off my saddle, got down and tied it to the hind legs, then threw it over the limb. I picked up the end of the lariat and jumped back on Betty, took my two wraps around the saddle horn again, and spoke to Betty. This time she really had to pull. She lifted that hog right up into the air to the limb.

Now, I wondered, will she hold it there until I can jump down, grab the other rope and tie it around the trunk of the tree to hold it? She did. I had it tied and could loose the other rope from the horn.

I fastened one short rope to a foreleg, threw it over the limb, took hold of it and pulled the front end of the hog up towards the limb. I got my shoulder under it and pulled and lifted. Soon the hog was hanging horizontal to the limb. I tied the rope, led Betty under the hog, then let it down into the saddle. Now it was just a matter of tying the hog tight in the saddle.

I did this by taking the lariat off the hog, doubling it to get the center. I threw two half hitches over the horn, threw a half

Wild hog

hitch around the body of the hog and pulled it tight, and ran the end of the rope down through the lower cinch ring and tied it. I did the same on the other side.

I reached down to pet Happy, who had been watching me so closely. "Piffle," I said. "Happy, that really took some doing." I led Betty over to the other pig. It was much smaller and I could pick it up and throw it up on top of the big hog. I tied it down the same way. I picked up Betty's reins and looked at Happy.

"Now, let's go home."

Another day, another adventure, and a lot of excitement for me and my dog. One good shot—in this case two shots—then a lot of hard work, but it was all exciting and worth it. We had a lot of good meat to salt cure and smoke for delicious hams and bacon and a small hog for fresh roasts and chops.

I came down into the flat and walked up to the cabin. Dad was cutting wood. "By jingoes, you got one," he said.

"Say Dad, you better look again."

"Well I'll be darned if you don't have *two* hogs on there.

Gee! that young one will make some great pork roasts. Where in the world did you find 'em?"

"Happy found them out in timber on the north side of Fir Mountain."

"How in the world did you get that big one loaded?"

"Well, I'll tell you it took some thinking, some doing, and a good horse to accomplish it." Later, I explained all the details. That evening, after a dinner of liver smothered in onions and mashed potatoes, brown gravy, a can of green beans and fresh hot baked biscuits, what could be better than hunting stories around the glowing coals of a fire?

CHAPTER 12

THE WILD RIDE

Walter came the following Friday, and I told him I'd like to go back with him Sunday afternoon. I hadn't been to town for months.

"Good idea, Leona. Why don't you plan on coming back Thursday in the truck? Dean and his friend, Pat, have been driving me crazy asking when they can get up to Aunt Nono's to go hunting. I can come back Friday evening and spend the weekend, then the boys and I will return Sunday afternoon."

I had plenty of meat, so Walter and I didn't go hunting. Instead, we helped Dad finish clearing out the garden area, now that we had seed to plant in it. Sunday afternoon came and we hiked up to the car.

I spent three days in town visiting friends. First I saw Irv and Beulah Berry. I also spent one evening with Fern and Guy Chapman and their two small daughters, Joyce and DeeDee. Fern's sister, Minnie Huckaby, lived with Guy and Fern. She was practically blind. We all called her Aunt Mimmie. She knew every one of us by our voices. She was always so cheerful, we all loved her. The girls often came to the homestead with Walter, and always called him Uncle Dick.

When Thursday afternoon came, the boys were raring to go. They had their guns ready. We piled into the cab of the truck and drove over to Fern's store where I bought some groceries and tied them on the back of the truck. The boys were elated that they were going to be out of school for two days.

The trip grew interesting after we left the main road at Las Lomas, because we started to see deer. The boys were trying to spy a big buck and they counted all the deer they could see. As we approached the steep hill past the old orchard, I slowed, put it in low gear and started down. I'd made this trip many times, so I thought nothing of it.

Soon the truck began going faster and faster. The back wheels were bouncing all over the road, back and forth! "Nono! Nono! What's the matter with the truck?" the boys yelled.

"I don't know!" I screamed. "But you better start praying like you never prayed before!"

The back end of the truck kept bouncing up and down and back and forth all over the road, but I managed to keep the truck on the road and finally got it stopped when I hit the level stretch.

I set the brake, put the gears in reverse, shut off the motor, and jumped out. The boys came flying around the back end. They looked at me, then hollered, "Whoo-ee! That was some ride!"

"Why'd the truck do that?" Pat asked.

"Yeah," Dean said. "What made it go so crazy?"

I was shaking in my boots and couldn't answer right away. Finally I said,"We don't have big racks on the truck, so there isn't enough weight on the bed of the truck to hold the wheels down. The momentum started 'em bouncing."

We walked around for a little while until I'd stored up enough courage to try the last of the grade.

"Ready to go?" I asked.

"Yeah," Dean said.

"Let's get it over with," Pat said.

"Tell you what I want you to do. Both of you jump up on the tail end of the truckbed and sit with your feet hanging over. Each of you take a big deep breath of air. That'll make you heavy enough to hold down the wheels. And don't jump off!"

I don't know if they appreciated my joke, but they ran around and scrambled up onto the bed of the truck. I climbed into the cab and hollered, "Ready?"

"Yeah!" Dean yelled.

I started off slow. Everything went fine, no more trouble and I soon pulled into the pack station. The boys jumped down and yelled, "Whoopee! We made it!"

I climbed down from the cab. "Thank goodness! I don't want *that* to happen again."

I could easily see my mistake. Whenever I'd driven down the grade before, I had had the big stock racks and end gates on the truck. They probably put four hundred or more pounds on the bed, and held the back wheels down.

We divided the groceries, the boys picked up their rifles, and we hiked to the cabin. Another day, another lesson learned. You can bet your bottom dollar I never again drove down the road without the racks on.

CHAPTER 13

THE BOW AND ARROW HUNTERS

The boys and I went hunting but didn't find anything. Dean's dad arrived Friday night and they all went back Sunday afternoon.

The week went by fast. Saturday morning was cold. We'd just finished breakfast when Happy started to bark. We looked out the little window I had built in the door, and there were two horseback riders coming up the trail. They rode right up to the door. One was Frank Fry's son, Ralph.

I said, "Hello Ralph, aren't you out early?"

"Morning," Dad said. "It's cold. Better come in. Leona will give you some hot coffee."

Ralph introduced his partner, Zeke, a friend from Santa Rosa whom everyone called High Pockets. I could see why he was saddled with that name when he got off his horse. He was six foot six and very slender.

"Gee," he said. "Hot coffee. Best thing I've heard all morning."

I made a fresh pot and we sat around the table drinking and talking. Ralph said to Dad, "We brought our bows and arrows, and wonder if you and Leona would go hog hunting with us."

"Too cold for me, Ralph, and we only have the one horse, but I bet Leona would like to go."

"Sure I'll go. I have a bow, too, you know. It'd be a good idea to have a rifle in the crowd, though, so I'll take mine."

"Good idea," Ralph said.

"I'll fix lunch."

"That's not necessary, Leona. Zeke and I have lunch enough for all of us."

"Then I'll get my warm coat on and saddle my horse and bring her up here."

When I got back to the cabin, the boys and Dad were outside. I handed Dad Betty's reins and went in to pick up my gun. I also picked up some short pieces of rope and a grain sack. I rolled up the sack and tied it on behind my saddle. We mounted up and said good-bye to Dad. "Don't look for us back until some time in the afternoon."

The horses were cold and anxious to be on the way. We rode out over Fir Mountain. Happy was with us, of course, and excited about going hunting. We didn't find any pig rooting, even after we had ridden clear down to the low divide between Cedar Creek and Danfield Creek. We stopped to talk over what we should do.

"I've never been down this far," Ralph said.

"What do we do now?" Zeke asked.

"I suggest we ride up over the divide to our left and drop into the Danfield, cross the creek and ride up Oak Mountain a ways."

"Leona, if Oak Mountain means anything, there ought to be a lot of acorns up there."

"Maybe you have something there, Ralph, let's give it a try."

We crossed the creek and started the climb up the side of Oak Mountain. We rode up about half way, through a lot of black oak, white oak and tan oak trees, then I suggested we work around to the southeast side where the sun was shining. "Hogs like a warm place to lay up for the day. Now we're getting into some manzanita, too."

We rode into a small opening surrounded by manzanita, and Happy took off around the hill. She started to bark, so I said, "Happy sounds like she's coming this way. Quick! Get off, tie your horses and get ready to shoot."

I jumped off my horse, threw the reins down, pulled my gun out and levered a cartridge into the barrel. A big black hog burst right through the little opening, running. Both boys shot at it with bows and arrows and missed. He headed straight for me.

I threw up my gun, took quick aim and fired. He was practically upon me! I had to jump aside to keep from being knocked down when he fell—hit by my bullet.

"Now, that's something," Zeke yelled. "Look at the *size* of that son of a gun. And it all happened so fast!"

As soon as Happy made sure the hog was dead, she was off again. This time she ran down the hill and in no time was baying again.

"Hurry up and get down there before the hog breaks and runs!" I yelled to the boys.

They charged down the hill and one of them got it with an arrow. Happy had bayed it up against a big fir log. It was a nice hog. Now Happy was gone again. We heard her baying up the hill quite a ways above us.

"Hurry up, kids, get up there and get it!"

In a little bit, I heard them hollering, "For God's sake, call off your dog! We'll have so many hogs we'll never get them packed out of here!"

Before I got up to them, Happy was gone again. This time she was away up on the mountain, roaming around and barking excitedly. We rushed up and came out into a big space of wet open grassland. Happy was chasing a small pig round and round and up and down. It wouldn't stop and bay up, and she wouldn't catch it and hold it.

"I'm going to catch it alive!" Zeke yelled, running after it. Ralph and I just collapsed on the ground with laughter as the gangly Zeke, Happy and the pig went around and around. Zeke's feet would fly out from under him when he turned short on the slick wet ground. Then he'd get up and go after the pig again. We really didn't know who was going to give out first, the pig or Zeke. We laughed until we had pains in our sides. Finally Zeke fell down on it, and when he got up he had it in his arms. He staggered over to us, so out of breath he could hardly talk.

Ralph and I had laughed so hard our sides still hurt. It was so funny to see that big tall boy running after that poor little pig. We sat there until Zeke could get his breath.

Zeke said, "I'm going to take this pig home with me and raise it." The little red-haired pig weighed about 25 or 30 pounds.

I said, "It will take awhile to get used to you, but it probably will grow into quite a large hog in about six months. Be sure you put it in a tight pen, or it will be gone the first morning."

We hiked back down to the horses, and I untied the rolled-up grain sack and gave it to Zeke. "Let's put the little pig in here," I said.

"Say, that's just the thing. You even brought a little rope to tie it with."

"The sack's open weave will let the pig breathe right through it."

Ralph strode over to his horse, untied the lunch and brought it over. We all sat down, even Happy, and ate heartily. The boys saw that Happy got her share, too.

"We have a quite a job now," I said. "We have to dress these hogs and get them on the horses."

We finally got that job done and led our horses back to the cabin. The boys were still jabbering about the hunt. "Imagine getting all these hogs, and with bows and arrows, too!" Zeke said.

"Yeah," I said. "It'll be a long time before you have another hunt like this."

"That's right, Leona," Ralph said. "I've hunted quite a few hogs, but never had a hunt like this one."

"You know who the big hero is," I said.

"Yeah, it's Happy. Where would we be without her? Stands to reason, we certainly wouldn't have all these hogs."

We took our time getting back to the cabin. Dad came out to greet us: "My land! where in the world did you find all those hogs?"

While I was making coffee, the boys took my horse over to the tree where we always hung up the hogs. When they came in, they told Dad the story as we sat around the table drinking coffee and eating cookies I'd baked to go with it.

Whenever I got a big fat hog like this one, I always made smoked sugar-cured ham and bacon out of it, and we'd have plenty to last us well into the summer.

Now it was getting late and the boys had to start for home. Dad said to Zeke, "Let us know how heavy the little red pig is when you sell it."

High Pockets lived on a ten-acre chicken ranch outside Santa Rosa. He had a good place to keep the little pig. We heard through Ralph many months later that the little red pig weighed over three hundred pounds when he finally sold it.

CHAPTER 14

THE LITTLE MULE

Walter had something interesting to tell me on Friday when he arrived at the cabin.

"Leona, I ran into your neighbor, Elmer Brown, in Santa Rosa the other day and we had quite a long visit. He asked about you and Dad. I told him about your homestead, and he said he had a little mule, a dandy little pack animal that will pack almost anything but is just too small to pack Elmer's heavy stock saddle and him all day long. If you want to use him, all you have to do is go over to his ranch and get him. He's well broken to ride or pack and he's so small he requires little hay and grain."

"A mule might be a big help around here, Walter."

"Oh, my, it would be great. We'd each have an animal to ride. What do you think, Dad?"

"Gee! I think it would be fine. When you go up to the pack station you could lead him in to pack and ride Betty back.

Dean's Easter vacation starts in a couple of weeks. He'd like to spend it up here. Why couldn't you and Dean go over and get him then?"

When Dean and his dad came up, we all worked around the cabin. "Walter," I said, "I think Monday would be a good day for Dean and me to go over to Elmer's ranch and get the mule."

"Gee! Aunt Nono, can I ride him home?" Dean asked.

"Sure, if you want to, but you'll have to ride him bareback as we only have the saddle for Betty."

"I don't mind riding bareback. It'll be fun."

Monday morning early, I saddled Betty and we started out for Elmer's place across the mountains towards the coast. I had never ridden through this country, but from the tops of the ridges we could see the ranch. Elmer had girdled many trees to kill them and open up grassland for his sheep. You could see the ranch from miles and miles away. Dean and I took turns riding and walking. It was a good twelve miles up and down hill, and we arrived just before lunch.

Elmer was out on the range looking after the sheep. Mrs. Brown, whom I'd previously met, was home. She greeted us, asked us in and wanted to know if we would eat lunch with her.

Of course, Dean said, "Gee, that sounds good to me."

I said, "Thanks, that would be fine." After lunch we visited for a while, then I said, "We have a long way to go. Guess we'd better be on our way."

"Yes, Elmer told me about The Cedars. That's where your homestead is, isn't it? I've never ridden that far. Let's go out to the barn and I'll lead the little mule out. I'll get his bridle too; his head is so small no other bridle will fit him."

When she led him out of the barn, I said, "Gosh, he's small, isn't he?"

"That's why Elmer doesn't like to ride him. Says he feels sorry for him and finds himself walking half the time."

"Can a person ride him bareback?" I asked.

"Oh yes, he's gentle and well broken. Our neighbor's girl has ridden him for a couple of years to grammar school. One thing I'll tell you about, don't ever turn him loose without a long rope on him or you'll never catch him. He's broken to a fifty- foot stake rope."

Mrs. Brown put the bridle on him and handed the reins to Dean. "I presume you're going to ride him?"

"You bet," Dean said.

"Oh, I forgot to tell you, his name is Jimmy." I thanked her and mounted up and turned around to watch Dean jump up on the little mule's back. Jimmy just exploded. He gave two big bucks across the yard and Dean found himself flat on the ground on the other side of him, or where he had been.

Dean picked himself up, looking kind of funny, wondering where he was hurt, or if he was hurt. The first words he said were: "Gosh all fish-hooks. I'm not getting on *that* critter again!"

"Oh, for heaven's sake, Dean! What kind of a cowboy are you? You going to let a little animal like that bluff you out?"

"I don't care. I'm not getting on that jumping jackass again, even if I have to *walk* home."

"Oh piffle," I said. "I'll take the saddle off Betty, shorten the cinch so it'll fit, and put it on Jimmy. You can ride Betty bareback. I'll bet Jimmy doesn't do a thing."

He didn't. He just plodded off as though it was the only way to go. I later found out he had a great many things stored away in that little head with long ears. He wasn't born to be a mule for nothing. He was small, only chest high to me, and I was five feet seven and a half. Jimmy had a glossy brown coat of hair with a black stripe that ran up one foreleg, over his back and down the other leg. He also had a black stripe all the way down the top of his back to the root of his funny little mule tail.

I thanked Elmer's wife again and headed for home. Everything went fine until we started down Oak Mountain. Then the saddle started slipping up onto his little withers. I had to stop and resaddle him every quarter of a mile. I pulled the cinch up so tight I thought it would cut him in two. I should've used a narrow-built saddle on him, or a pony saddle. He was very small and had narrow withers.

We arrived at the cabin just before dark. Dad saw us coming over the rocky ridge and waited for us out in the yard. As we rode up, he said, "Say! you did get a *little* saddle animal! If I ever ride him my feet will drag on the ground."

"Oh Dad, I have it all figured out. You can put a plowshare on each boot and plow out the trail as you ride."

"My land, that just might be an idea," Dad chuckled, but I don't think he ever rode Jimmy.

As Elmer had promised Walter, Jimmy was extremely easy to keep. He wouldn't eat more than a pint of barley at one time. Horses have no sense about grain. They'll keep eating until they founder themselves. It's really bad when that happens, because they get quite sick and, even when they get over it, their muscles are always stiff first thing in the morning. After they travel a ways and warm up, then they're all right.

Jimmy took a great liking to Betty and wanted to have her in his sight at all times. Whenever he couldn't see her, he'd let out an ear-splitting bray. It sounded like a bullfrog in distress, only about ten times faster on the croak.

Little Jimmy had another surprise for me the first time I saddled him by the cabin and headed him down the flat. As soon as I put my foot in the stirrup and started to swing up into the saddle, he took off on a dead run, and I came up *behind* the saddle. It's a wonder I didn't fall off his darned small rump, but I had a good hold on the reins and jerked him up and was able to stop him.

"If that's the way you want to play," I said, "I'll just play a little harder with you."

Next time I was ready for him. I had a short hold on the reins, and his bridle had a severe ring bit on it, and when I swung up into the saddle I pulled right quick on the reins. It was not a gentle pull either. I nearly sat him on his haunches. The bit really hurt his mouth. He never pulled that stunt with me again; he was quick to learn.

Another habit he had really exasperated me. When I tied him to a tree and turned to walk away he would lunge forward and bite me in the middle of the back. It hurt like fury and a time or two made a big blood blister. "This has to stop," I said to myself. "I'll fix you." I cut a stick about sixteen inches long, similar to a policeman's billy-club.

I tucked this under my left arm the next time I tied him up and started to walk off. I watched him out of the corner of my eye and when he lunged at me I came down across his nose with the billy-club. Boy, was he ever surprised! I carried the

Hay-bale packsaddle on Jimmy

stick with me for a while but he never did that with me again. He was smart in lots of ways, some good and some bad.

He used to bluff men out. They'd come walking in leading Jimmy, whose little thinking cap must've told him, "Humans have two legs to walk on. Why should I pack them if I can get away without them?"

On different occasions I have seen him bite, rear up on his hind feet and strike with his front feet, then whirl around and kick. He was well broken, but you had to ride him with a firm hand and let him know who was boss. And yet a small child could ride him and he wouldn't do anything bad.

He was an interesting little animal. He would stand patiently while I packed things onto him, and he never tried to buck anything off. His little hooves were hard and I only had him shod once, on his hind feet. I rode him for fifteen years, and during that time I was riding long days and working cattle. He was good at cutting cattle in the corral.

CHAPTER 15

WILDFLOWERS

My brother usually came up every third or fourth weekend and brought the groceries I had requested the trip before. He would leave the groceries in the car at the pack station and walk in to the cabin. The next day I would ride up on Betty or Jimmy to get them.

We didn't need a great many groceries, since we got all our meat from the land. The garden was beginning to provide us with vegetables. In the spring we had all the trout we wanted and I also shot a lot of young grouse. They tasted as good as young fryer chickens. August and September was deer season. We had plenty of venison and I usually made a lot of jerky. I really liked that for lunches. After the first rain, I could find hogs again. Then around Christmastime the steelhead swam up the creeks. We had quite a variety in our meat shop in the woods.

I enjoyed springtime, not only for its good weather, but so many wildflowers began to pop up out of the ground. The trees, especially the black oaks, were all bursting out in new pink and green leaves. Azaleas were thick up and down the creeks. I would sit in the doorway of the cabin smelling the sweet aroma of the azaleas.

When I rode out over the mountain, I found hound's tongue, baby blue eyes and, once in a while in the early spring, I'd see a bright red spot in the manzanita. When I made my way over to it, I'd be greeted by a fire-red snow plant. One day in a tiny creek with a little waterfall, I found a charming orchid about ten inches tall, standing there just close enough to get a slight mist from the waterfall. The petals were light to deep rose in color with a sprinkling of brownish pink to mottled purple. When I arrived back at the cabin it was fun to take the *California Wild Flower* book and look it up. It was a very rare wild orchid called Calypso.

All through the spring there were mission bells, fawn lilies and Indian paint brushes as well as the taller, sturdier Indian warriors, columbine, Diogenes' lanterns, pussy willows, clarkia, false lady slipper, tiger lilies, spice bush and dogwood trees. I could go on and on. There were many more colorful creations of nature's paint brush.

I think the greatest wild flower show I ever saw in my life was one weekend when my brother came up to visit. He said, "Leona, let's take our fishing rods tomorrow morning and walk over to Cedar Creek and catch a nice mess of trout."

"Fine," I said. "You know me, I'm always ready to go trout fishing."

After breakfast, Walter said, "I'll go down to the manure pile and get some nice big angle worms."

"Fine. There's a Prince Albert tobacco can in the tree by my saddle. Put my worms in that; it fits nicely in my shirt pocket. I'll make a couple of sandwiches apiece to tuck in the back of our shirts to carry us over until we get back."

We picked up our rods, told Dad goodbye and promised, "We'll bring home some nice trout for dinner."

"I'll have the fire going," Dad said.

As we crossed the rocky ridge, we saw several deer out feeding, so we stopped to watch them for a little while, then went on our way. Instead of taking the saddle trail, as soon as we got on the Cedar Creek side of the mountain, we angled down around the base of Fir Mountain towards the creek. As we hiked down closer to the creek we came to a sidehill of scattered oak where the ground was very damp and spongy.

All of a sudden we saw an acre or more of orchids in a solid mass of blossoms. We were so surprised we could hardly believe our eyes. The most Walter or I had ever seen in one place had been one or two clumps, and here was a whole sidehill of a rare mountain flower, a member of the orchid family named Mountain Lady Slipper.

The clumps were twenty to thirty inches tall and nearly all were in bloom. The blossoms looked like little Dutch wooden shoes. Each blossom was white and two to two-and-a-half inches long with purple streaks running from the heel along the side of the blossom and up over the toe. It was such an unusual sight we started counting the blossoms on one clump. There were thirty-two of those little delicate slippers. It was a tremendous show.

I looked at Walter. "Why haven't we a camera? How I'd *love* to have a picture of this! No one will ever believe us when we tell them about it."

"We don't even have a camera back at the cabin. Remember when we were over at Las Lomas, if we found a blossom or two, we only picked one blossom to take home to Mother? We were afraid it would kill the plant if we picked both flowers. She loved all the wildflowers so much. Wonder what she'd have thought if she could've seen something like this?"

"Guess if we're going to have trout for dinner tonight, Walter, we better be on our way."

"Yeah, we can't eat these flowers."

Reluctantly, we left the beautiful hill of orchids and continued on down to the creek, then baited our hooks. Walter took his pocket knife and cut a couple of small limbs of pepperwood about twenty-four inches long and trimmed off the branches, all but the bottom one, and left that one about four inches long. He gave me one. Now we had something to string our trout on.

We started fishing down the creek and just kept the largest trout, nine to twelve inches long. The smaller ones, if they weren't hurt, we threw back. We stopped at noon and sat down to enjoy our sandwiches and listen to the stream as it gurgled its way to the ocean. Five-fingered ferns grew thick along the banks of the creek, with hosts of delicate maidenhair fern.

We fished until our pepperwood switches were full of nice fish. Then Walter said, "Better head for home. Sun's getting low."

We picked some damp ferns and rolled the trout in them to keep them cool and prevent them from drying out and placed them in our lunch sacks.

A divide rose to our left. I said, "Let's head that way. There should be a saddle trail going up the ridge towards Fir Mountain."

We hiked up to the divide and indeed there was a worn trail that led toward Fir Mountain, so we took our time walking. We jumped a few deer out of little patches of brush as we walked by, including bucks with small horns. There were no wild pigs around, but we didn't want one, anyway. Walter had his .45 Colt pistol on his belt, just in case.

We finally reached the top of the little rocky ridge just above the cabin flat, them paused and looked back. The sun was disappearing behind Fir Mountain like a big red ball of fire. The sky, a soft reddish hue, was full of fleecy white clouds. A beautiful sight.

Dad had a good fire going. It didn't take me long to prepare supper of fried trout, boiled potatoes, canned corn, and good fresh-made coffee. For dessert we ate canned peaches.

We told Dad about the huge patch of Lady Slippers. He said, "Too bad your mother couldn't have seen that. She would've loved it."

"Yes, she loved nature so much. She would've enjoyed our fishing trip today, too."

CHAPTER 16

THE NEW ROOM

The days were getting longer and warmer, and we were gathering radishes, small beets and carrots from the garden. The first thing each morning, the sun's rays peeped over the ridge and warmed the soil in the garden. It was warm enough to plant corn, and the string beans would need sticks shoved in the ground to run up on.

It was time to build another room onto the cabin. We had been able to live quite comfortably in one room and had survived the winter in good shape. But I was getting tired of cooking on dear old Hazel, with no oven for baking cookies and cakes, although I was able to bake bread on top of the stove.

I had a nice little four-hole regular cookstove up at the pack station. It had an oven, too, and I knew it was a good baker, because Winona and I had used it. We'd bought it when we started high school in Healdsburg. Dad and Mother had rented two rooms for us and we kept house there.

I wanted to build on a kitchen and a small bedroom for my room. We talked about this and decided to dig the hill back a little farther. Then I could build the room sixteen feet long, big enough to measure off about eight feet on the north end for a small bedroom for me. I had an old windshield half that was in good shape, and I figured I could frame it into the two-foot addition on the northwest wall. In the north end, I would partition off a small room for my bedroom.

The kitchen would be added on in the south end and

measure eight feet by eight feet. I had a small four-pane window I could frame into the south wall just to the left of where the little cook stove would stand. In the middle of the day, it would let the winter sun in for a while.

That evening after dinner, I said, "I'd like to get started. First we have to make the shakes."

"Why can't we take the tools and go out and saw some cuts off the fir log?" Dad said. "You know how to split shakes."

"Let's start on it tomorrow, Dad."

"While you split out the shakes, I'll pack 'em in. I'll pack Jimmy and ride Betty. I'll be in style."

"In a couple of days I can get enough shakes split out. It'll take longer to get the four foundation logs and the poles for the frame work. I'll build it just like we built the first room, except for the walls. There'll have to be a pole nailed around the room three feet up from the floor. The boards will only be three feet long, same as the shakes. I'll nail two rows of three-foot boards on the sides to make the six foot height. It won't look quite as nice, but then, who's to see it?"

Next morning after a substantial breakfast of home cured ham, hot cakes and syrup, and coffee, we saddled Jimmy and Betty. Walter had brought up a saddle he had at his place, so we were all set. It was nice to have two saddle animals. We took our tools out with us and figured we'd ride back for lunch.

We rode out over the flat and down to the fir log. I staked Jimmy out with the lariat and pulled his bridle off, and Dad took Betty's bridle off and put a halter on her and let her drag her rope. There was a lot of bunch grass here for them to breakfast on. Besides, this saved on the hay we'd otherwise pack in.

We each took hold of a handle of the saw and started a cut three feet from the sawed-off end of the log. Dad had sharpened the saw so it spat out long shavings. We sawed off several cuts. I started driving a row of wedges across the log and we took turns pounding them in. It didn't take long to

burst the cut open. It was a good splitting tree, thank goodness.

With a marker and a piece of chalk, I marked out the shake
bolts, then picked up a wedge and split them out. Now I was
ready to stand a bolt on end and split my shakes.

I drove two stakes in the ground about two feet high and
twenty inches apart and tied them together with a piece of tie
wire. I set the bolt up in front of the wire. As I split each shake
off with the froe, it lay over against the wire. By doing it this
way, each shake fell back against the previous shake, so it
made a nice tight bundle. When I had twenty-five, I wired
them tight together with a piece of baling wire. That was one
bundle.

The boards were split with the grain the other way, so
they were smoother.

After I had made up a few bundles of shakes, Dad got
Jimmy and started to pack them on the saddle. I helped him,
for it was difficult to insert the bundles in the rope loops on
the saddle. Ordinarily we should have been using a regular
pack saddle and two iron hooks that fit on the saddle. They
would have been much simpler to load. Dad soon had a load
for Jimmy. Now he could ride Betty and lead Jimmy.

I kept on splitting shakes and boards. By the time he
returned I had another load split, tied, and ready for him. I
helped him load. By the afternoon of the second day we had a
nice lot of building material piled up by the cabin. "Dad," I
said, "I think I have enough to build my room."

The third day, we scouted the hillside just above the cabin
and found the best trees for foundation logs. We sawed and
chopped them down and trimmed them. I put Betty to work
as I saddled her and threw two half hitches around the end of
the log and had her pull it by the saddle horn. The logs were
much smaller than the ones we had put in the other room. I
cut them ten feet long. I had to have four of them plus two
short ones. Then I cut twelve six-foot posts for the so-called
two by fours for the wall. They were small, so Dad chopped

them down and I trimmed. We cut six for plates and ten poles for rafters.

It took us a couple of days to trim, cut and drag the logs down to the cabin. Monday morning, I laid the foundation logs, then put up my cornerposts and wall posts. Now came the horizontal plates at top and bottom to nail the boards to. I made a space in the center back wall for a back door, which would have the biggest posts. I spliced the top plate on them as it was impossible to get a sixteen-foot pole. In the two-foot addition on the northwest side I framed in the half windshield.

I was ready to nail the boards on the wall. I had fitted the pole where the three foot boards had to overlap halfway up the wall by chopping a notch in the upright poles. Now I did the same with the poles that were nailed halfway up. This made the framework all even . The only irregularity that would show would be the overlap. The wall looked fairly straight after all.

After I had the walls up and closed in, I set the ridgepole in the center and braced it until I could get some of the rafters nailed to it. Rather than saw all the angles to fit the rafters to the ridgepole, I just flattened the underside with a hatchet and extended the rafters onto the ridgepole. That's the way Walter and I had placed the rafters in the main room.

It worked out very well. Now I nailed the sheeting or cross poles, flattening them some where they fit over the rafters. Soon I was ready to start nailing shakes.

Shakes make a nice-looking roof, and they go on fast, so I enjoyed the work. As before, I cut the bundles in half for the starter row at the base of the roof, then laid a row of full length shakes over that. One has to be careful and lay the second shake so it is centered over the joint of the lower row. The outside edge is filled in with shakes split in half. This makes a long-lasting roof. The ends of the shakes are exposed eleven inches to the weather, and the nails are under the overlap of the next shake so there are no nails exposed to the weather to rust, and let rain seep in. The overlay makes the roof three shakes thick. If the house doesn't burn down, a redwood roof is good for fifty years of wear from the rain. I really didn't know how long the fir shakes would last, but I imagined it would be good for many years.

The edge of the roof on the back side of the cabin was only about four feet off the ground. When I was nailing on the roof shakes, Happy sat on the sidehill and looked up at me, as if to say, "Why are you way up there?" Then she had the bright idea of jumping on the roof and scrambling up to me.

Happy'd had a litter of puppies early in the spring, and I'd given all but one pup away. The father was a male dog that Frank Fry brought around one day; at least, I guess that's when Happy decided it was time to raise a family. Dad had some bales of hay stacked down the flat, and one morning I walked down there and heard this funny kind of squeaking. When I investigated, I found six little black and white puppies. I kept them until they were six weeks old.

Walter came up one weekend and I said, "I have to get rid of these puppies. I'm going to keep one, but if you took them down home with you maybe Dori and Dean would take care of them until they could give them away."

"I'm sure Dean could give them away. He's told the kids at school about coming up here and hunting hogs with Happy. Some of the boys probably would be glad to get her puppies."

When Walter and I rode up to his car Sunday afternoon, we carried the puppies in two grain sacks in front of us in the saddle. I watched Walter drive off, then I headed for home, riding Betty and leading Jimmy. In many other ways too, Jimmy was saving all of us from a lot of walking.

Next morning when I started nailing shakes, Happy jumped up on the roof to join me. At first, her puppy sat on the ground and whined, but the next thing I knew the pup was up on the roof too, scrambling, slipping, sliding, digging in with toenails until it was above me, then sliding down into my lap.

"How in the world am I supposed to do anything with

you two in the way? What are you doing up here?" The more I talked to them, the faster their tails wagged, mostly in my face. "I just can't do anything with you two pests in my way. Why don't you go down and play, or chew on a bone, or pester Dad to throw a stick for you."

Finally I had to get stern with them and use a tone of voice they knew meant business. "Go on! Get out of here! Just move out of here. Slide down off here!"

They got the picture and slid off the roof. They sat down on the hillside and looked up at me and let out a couple of little barks, as if to say, "She's such an old meanie!"

They finally decided they'd find Dad and try to get him to throw some sticks to run after.

I loved my dogs and talked to them a great deal, especially Happy, who was such good company. I played hide-and-go-seek with them. Happy was always glad to see me pick up my rifle, sure we were going hunting. She seemed to know if it was in the winter it was hogs, in the deer season it was deer.

The pup wasn't old enough to go hunting. She didn't know enough to stay away from a hog and I was afraid she would meet up with an old boar with razor sharp tusks and that would be the end of her.

I've had several dogs badly cut up by a hog they had cornered. One upward thrust from a hog's tusk can rip a dog wide open. Then, too, when a dog has a hog bayed the action happens so fast that several ranchers have shot their own dogs by mistake. Thank goodness I never did that, but I did have a terrible experience over at the Las Lomas Ranch with Jack, an excellent hunting dog.

I had taken Mr. Bruhns and his wife out for a hog hunt. I knew them quite well. For several years, they had come up to Las Lomas from San Francisco to hunt deer. I carefully explained: "Never go downhill from the hog when the dog has it bayed, as it may charge you."

Jack rousted a big hog and bayed it in a fern patch close to the bottom of a ravine. As we jumped off our horses, of all things Mr. Bruhns dashed in below the fern patch. The hog charged him, the dog hot on his heels right behind him. He shot the hog and killed it instantly, but the bullet zipped through the hog's head, hit the dog in his ear, passed through his neck, into his shoulder, hitting the shoulder blade before glancing out.

"Oh my God! I've killed Leona's dog!" he hollered. Hog and dog came tumbling down into the ravine. The dog was knocked out, and lying there bleeding badly. Now Mr. Bruhns was crying and his wife was crying.

About that time the dog came to and staggered to his feet. "Come on, the dog isn't dead," I said. "Let's get something to stop the blood!"

Mr. Bruhns ripped off his coat, shirt and undershirt. "Here take these if you need 'em—anything to save the dog." The Bruhnses stopped crying and tried to stanch the dog's bleeding and make him as comfortable as possible. They proposed taking the dog to a veterinarian in San Francisco. But I said the wound was more or less a flesh wound, so I figured Jack would be all right with my own medical care.

I dressed the hog, we loaded it on the horse, and then I lifted the dog up in the saddle with me for the ride home. Mrs. Bruhns rode her horse and her husband walked and led the horse bearing the hog.

The Bruhnses stayed that night with us, and next morning Jack was up and walking around, so I told them he'd be all right. They helped me cut up the hog and wrap it and took most of it home with them. Jack survived and hunted many hogs after that. The Bruhnses came back to hunt, but always hunted deer.

I've been chased up a tree or two myself, especially when I had no gun. I even had one hog charge my saddle horse when I rode in below it. Luckily the horse jumped out of the way. The charging hog just goes on, and doesn't turn around to fight. I guess that's one thing that makes hunting so exciting—one never knows just what might happen.

Happy was smart about rattlesnakes, too. She always let me know when one was around. I think she could smell a rattler at least a hundred yards away. One day Dad and I were in the cabin eating lunch and we heard Happy baying something. I jumped up from the table, grabbed my rifle and rushed out the door. She was around on the north side of the cabin, so I ran around there and saw a big rattlesnake against the wall, coiled up and striking at her as she jumped around, barking. I got a chance to shoot and plugged it in the head, killing it. Dad was right behind me with a shovel in case it was needed. A shovel or hoe is a pretty good tool to kill a rattler with.

Happy was smart enough not to go close to the rattlesnake, as a rattler can still bite even after being shot to pieces. Dad scooped this one up on his shovel and took him off somewhere and buried him.

After we settled down to finish our lunch, Dad said, "That was a big rattlesnake! Did you see it striking at Happy?"

"Sure wouldn't want him striking at me. It was a good lesson for the puppy, too. I noticed she stayed away from it and did her share of barking."

"There'll be another one around here, because they always travel in pairs. I'll watch for him and carry my shovel with me."

A week later, Dad was hoeing in the garden, and he found the second rattlesnake stretched out under the leaves in the beet row. He whacked its head off with the hoe, picked up his shovel, carried off the snake and its severed head, and buried them. Those were the only two rattlesnakes we ever saw on the flat by the cabin, although I killed plenty on the range or along the road as I drove to town.

CHAPTER 17

FINISHING THE ROOM

I went back to finish the new room, framing the doorway logs with smooth boards. Then I built a frame of small poles to fit the door opening and covered it with shakes. To make a hinge, I left the pole on the back of the door frame an inch-and-a-half longer than the door. I whittled the pole ends down to a small round peg, then bored a hole in the underside of the top, or header log, to take the top end of the pole. Then I bored a hole for the bottom end of the pole. In order to insert the top and bottom of the door hinge, I chiseled the side out of the lower hole. I slipped the top of the hinge pole in its hole and slid the bottom end into the bottom hole and nailed a wedge-shaped block against the pole on the bottom so it couldn't come out. The front door hinge worked the same way.

When I built the front door, I framed in a small four-pane window in the top half of the door. It gave us a view down the flat and across the top of the little rocky ridge. I made the latch out of a smooth piece of board eight inches long and two inches wide, then drilled a small hole in the latch board three inches from the front end. I tied a buckskin string to the latch, then drilled a small hole six inches above the level latch to put the string through and fastened the latch board to the door by driving a nail through the back end of the latch, creating a pivot for it to work up and down, door-knob high. I nailed two little blocks on the door close to the front edge. They were just a little thicker than the latch board. I nailed a small board

Construction of the door—from inside

over these blocks as a keeper for the latch. You could raise the latch and open the door from outside by pulling on the string.

The front end of the latch bar extended two inches past the edge of the door. I nailed a small block on the door jamb log in line with the level latch board. Over the block, I nailed a short board that extended above the block two inches. This gave the latch a notch to drop into. The latch was on the inside of the door and the latch string hung outside. Maybe that's where the saying, "Leave the latch string out for me," came from. To finish the door I nailed small straight strips of wood on the door casing on the outside of the door when it was shut. The door opened in, and when it was shut against these strips it stopped any drafts that might have come through the crack around the door.

We used the wheelbarrow to fill in the floor with dirt, then hauled in wheelbarrow loads of fine shale rock and tamped it in hard.

I laid a couple of layers of cardboard on the floor and laid linoleum over the cardboard. This floor was still in good shape when Dad and I moved out five years later. There's always a way to figure out how to do things.

Now it was time to go up to the pack station and fetch the cook stove. You might wonder, "How in the world can a person pack a stove in a saddle on a horse or mule?" Where there's a will, there's a way. I saddled Jimmy, Dad saddled Betty, and we rode up to the pack station. I dug the stove out from under the old canvas cover, took off all the lids and doors, removed the grates and placed them in two grain sacks that Dad held open for me. I tied them with a couple of pieces of rope, to hang on Dad's saddle horn. There was a small stack of baled hay in the corral. We took out one bale, cut the wires and divided the bale in half and rewired it.

I took the middle of my lariat and tied it to the saddle horn with two half-hitches. I threw a loop over the cantle of the saddle, pulled the loop down about half way on the skirt of the stirrup leather, picked up the end of the rope under the loop and ran it down through the lower cinch ring, then did the same on the other side.

Dad took hold of one end of the half bale of hay and I took hold of the other end. We placed it against the saddle so it was about one inch above the horn and one inch above the cantle, under the loop. I slipped the loop half way down on the hay,

picked up the end of the rope that was through the cinch ring
and brought it up through the loop, ran it back down to the
cinch ring, pulled it tight and tied it. We did the same on the
other side. This was called a blanket hitch and worked very
well.

Now there was a good flat place to set the stove on top of
the hay. It helped to get the mule on the downhill side; then
we didn't have to lift things so high. We took hold of the stove
and set it up on the hay. I threw the end of the rope over the
top of the stove, then went around on the far side and pulled
the rope tight and tied it to the cinch ring. I took the end of the
rope on that side and threw it over the stove, then walked
around and pulled it through the cinch ring and tied it.

I picked up Jimmy's lead rope and said, "Come on, let's
go." I guess this didn't make much sense to Jimmy but it
made me feel better. Dad rode behind Jimmy to watch the
load.

I headed up the trail with Jimmy right behind me and the
stove rocking along with the motion of his body. If a load is
properly balanced and tied down tight, it comes through with
no problems. I was always careful to balance a load.

Sometimes things go wrong. One time over at Las Lomas,
my sister Winona and I went deer hunting out on Big Mountain. I killed a nice three-point buck down on Morrel Creek
Ridge. We dressed it out and loaded it on my horse, Babe.
Rather than climb back up the mountain, we took the trail
down the ridge and dropped down into Toombs Creek. The
trail was steep here. Winona rode ahead of me. I was walking
and leading my horse. All of a sudden I was nearly jerked off
my feet. I looked back and Babe was standing there with the
saddle and deer under her belly. Any other horse would have
taken off and bucked until everything was loose or had broken off.

I yelled to Winona and she turned her horse around and
came back. She jumped off and helped me get the saddle
loose and the deer off. I resaddled Babe, then Winona and I

had to reload the deer. I really tied it down tight this time. I guess I hadn't pulled the cinch up tight enough.

It was not from lack of experience, either. One year my brother Walter and I cut and peeled thirty-two cords of tan-bark oak down in Wolf Creek Canyon. We had to pack it out on three horses, Babe, Bonnie and Betty, up to the road where it could be picked up by truck.

We packed the stove without a hitch and set it against the south wall of the cabin next to the window I'd put in. The stove was a dandy, especially with that hot manzanita wood. I found out I could bake biscuits in ten minutes.

I later packed in some finished lumber that Walter brought up to me. I built two cupboards on the wall with a counter under them, then cupboards below the counter. On the other wall I built a shelf for the water bucket and a bench for the wash basin, and of course a wood-box under the window.

Then I built a partition across the north end of the room with a door into my bedroom.

We carried our water from the creek that ran through the yard at the back of the cabin. Below, the falls made a big pool.

In the summer I went swimming every day. It was so cold it was quite a shock when I first went in. Naturally I didn't stay in very long, but oh, it was refreshing!

We carried all the water to put on the garden, but it really paid off. In late August we planted a winter garden of beets, carrots, cabbage, cauliflower and broccoli, and a few turnips.

Meat was hard to keep in the summer, so I made quite a bit of jerky—very good for lunches, along with dried prunes and walnuts.

All summer long I used the creek as my refrigerator. I put butter or whatever I wanted to be cold in mason jars and set them in the water in the shade. The running water kept everything cold. It really was not a bad way to live.

CHAPTER 18

THE DISHES AND THE PIG

The day after hauling the stove, I rode up to the pack station for a small tub of dishes I'd stored there.

Every trip was different. You could see deer or quail and, once in a while, a grouse. They made so much noise with their wings when they flew out of a tree. I tied Jimmy to the corral fence, crawled through the poles and pulled out a small bale of hay. I divided it in half and rewired it as before, and put each half bale on Jimmy, tying it on with the blanket hitch as before. Then I set the small tub of dishes on the top of the hay and tied it down to the cinch ring on each side of Jimmy.

"Come on Jimmy, let's go! We've got a big climb ahead of us."

I could have ridden Betty and led Jimmy up to pack the load back, but I guess I was just too lazy to saddle both animals. Anyway I liked to walk.

We made our way up the trail. It was well trimmed, so we didn't have to stop to get around trees. Almost at the top of the mountain Happy pointed her nose toward the sky and sniffed. I knew she'd scented something. She started around the mountain and headed for a side ridge. Soon I heard her bark, then her baying sound.

I tied Jimmy to a tree, pulled my rifle from the scabbard and pumped a shell into the chamber. I worked my way around the mountain through thick small cedars and found Happy had bayed a hog in a small opening on the top of the ridge. I waited until I had a chance for a good shot. One shot and the hog dropped, never knowing what had hit him.

Happy ran over to me. I petted her, then she ran back to the hog. As I walked, I told her she was such a good dog that I just didn't know what I'd do without her. Her tail wagged a mile a minute. She was always such a happy dog.

I hung the hog up in a tree. Fortunately, I had a rope long enough to get the hog off the ground. I tied the rope to one hind leg, threw the rope over a limb then pulled on the rope and shoved on the hog. I got it up far enough to dress it out. I knew I'd have to leave it there and thought it would be all right for the night.

I guessed its weight to be about one hundred pounds after it was dressed. I went back to Jimmy and we were on our way. When I arrived at the cabin door, Dad came out and helped me lift the tub down and carry it into the cabin. He took Jimmy down to his beloved Betty. You should have heard his melodious bray!

I unpacked the dishes and set them in the cupboard. I'd wash them all later. I had glasses and mason jars packed in paper. Not a one had even cracked.

When Dad came back from feeding Betty and Jimmy I told him what I had hanging up. "Shall we saddle the animals and go get it this evening?" he asked.

"No," I said. "I think it'll be all right. We'll go up tomorrow morning, right after breakfast. I have it dressed and hung up. I'm afraid we would be out after dark if we went tonight."

Next morning was cool and beautiful, a nice day for a ride. The deer also found it a good day to be out. We saw six as we rode up the trail, then a flock of mountain quail up ahead of us. They are colorful birds and much bigger than the valley quail. We were soon over the top of the mountain and down to the hog. We loaded it on Jimmy, tied it down and started back. Jimmy was used to carrying hogs or deer, and it didn't bother him one bit. I guess he thought it was just a natural thing to do; he wasn't silly like Betty. We hung the hog in the tree, then skinned it.

I bought kerosene for our lamps by the fifteen gallon drum for one dollar and fifty cents. Fifteen gallons lasted us all winter. I left the drum at the pack station, and when I wanted some I filled two glass gallon jugs and carried them in a grain sack hung from the saddle horn.

One day I rode up on Jimmy to fetch two gallons. I filled the jugs, pushed the corks in and hung the sacks over the horn, jumped in the saddle and started for the cabin. We'd gotten about halfway when Jimmy started dancing around, shying off the trail, first on one side then on the other, as if a bunch of yellow- jackets were after him.

"Jimmy, what in the world is the matter with you?"

Suddenly it dawned on me that maybe the jugs were leaking and the kerosene was seeping onto his skin and burning him. Sure enough, they'd been leaking. I unsaddled Jimmy, rubbed his shoulders as dry as I could with a bandana, and let the breeze blow on them for awhile before resaddling him. When I hung the jugs back on the saddle and mounted up, he took off and was his merry little self again.

This trail has many memories. Once while I was in Santa Rosa, Walter and I planned to go up to the claim after he was through work for the day. He was driving a school bus, and we left as soon as he put the bus away. It was dark when we drove into the pack station in Walter's Model A but we started walking. It was pitch black, no moon, and we didn't have a light of any kind.

That was the most horrible hike I ever took in my life. We stumbled over countless rocks and little tree stumps that we'd cut off when we trimmed out the trail to get through the first time. We fell down innumerable times and got up each time, only to do it all over again.

"We *have* to do something about this before there's a next time," I said to Walter.

"Sure do, Leona. I know just what to do, and I'll do it tomorrow. You got any empty lard pails at the cabin?"

"What for?"

"I'll show you tomorrow. Let's keep going and see if we can make it to the cabin."

Finally we reached the little rocky ridge, and we could glimpse the light from the little window in the cabin's front door. What a welcome sight that light was!

Next day Walter and I made miner's lanterns from two five-pound, lard pails. Walter showed me how to turn each handle so it connected the top to the bottom, which placed the open top of the pail facing forward and the bottom for reflecting light. With a heavy knife, we cut the hole to hold the candle in the bottom side of the bucket. That is, we cut sharp, pointed strips, and bent them up inside the pail. When Walter pushed a big white candle into the bucket, the sharp tin points gripped it firmly.

Now the lanterns were ready and they made a wonderful light to walk by. The light didn't shine in our eyes, yet it cast a good beam in front of our feet. The candle was so protected it never blew out in any kind of wind. We left our lanterns up at the pack station, and many times they proved to be worth their weight in gold when we had to find our way in on a dark night.

CHAPTER 19

THE BARN AND THE HAY

One evening after Dad and I quit work in the garden, we walked over to the creek bank to look back at all we had done.

"Dad," I had a thought, "We ought to think about building a shed before next winter, so Jimmy and Betty will have protection from heavy rainstorms."

"Yes, I hated to see Betty out and tied all last winter. When stock are loose they can seek shelter. They always stand tail to the storm."

It was almost the first of June but I shivered. "Let's go to the cabin. The sun's gone behind the mountain and it's chilly here on the creek bank." Back at the cabin I lit the Aladdin lamp and started supper.

"Leona, why don't we go out to our log lumber yard, split a bunch of boards and shakes and build a shed for the animals?"

"Why not? We can get started on it this week. We don't have anything special to do, do we?"

"No. Just give me a day to sharpen the saw."

"We could start the day after tomorrow and get something done this week."

After breakfast on Wednesday, Dad said, "I'll saddle Betty and Jimmy if you want to clear up the dishes."

Dad led the animals up to the cabin and we gathered our tools together and started out to the log. The sun was peeking up over the southeastern ridge, and the air was crisp and invigorating. A slight breeze drifted the fragrance of wild azalea bushes toward us. They were in blossom and prolific all along the creek bottom that bordered the edge of the flat.

We rode out the trail through scrubby manzanita. Several little brush rabbits went hopping away and I could see their little round, fluffy white tails disappearing into thicker hiding places. At the log, we unloaded our tools.

I said, "Dad, just for the fun of it, let's ride over the top of Fir Mountain out to the open ground."

"Sounds like a good idea."

We rode through a grove of thick Douglas fir mixed with pretty tan oaks, their new green leaves all shiny and smooth on one side, their undersides covered with a fine light yellow powder. Now we came out into the big open country.

The horses ambled out into the grass a little way, and Dad exclaimed, "Leona, look at the *height* of these wild oats! Why, they're clear up to my knees and I'm sitting on a horse!"

I jumped off Jimmy, waded out into the grass and looked down. "Dad, the ground's covered with burr clover under the oats."

"This'd make wonderful hay, but how in the world would we get it cut?"

"We have that big Italian scythe back at the cabin—no, I think it's still up at the pack station."

"Shoot, I could never make any progress with a scythe."

"Oh piffle! I think I can use it. At least, I could try."

"If you can cut it, I'll fork it into shocks so it'll cure and dry, but how will we get it to the cabin?"

"We could use those big alfalfa sacks up at the pack station. We could pack them tight and get three loaded to a horse. It wouldn't take long to pack in a ton or two of hay."

"Shall we let the boards go for a while and try the hay cutting?"

"Sure, let's do that. It certainly would be great to have a couple of tons of hay for next winter."

We went back to the log, and I staked Jimmy out on his fifty foot rope. Dad pulled Betty's bridle off and replaced it with her halter, then just let her drag her rope. Now they could fill up on bunch grass. While they ate breakfast, Dad and I sawed off several cuts, then split one in half. I marked out some bolts and split them. Now I stood one up against the wire frame, picked up the froe and mall, tipped the bolt back against my thigh and split off a shake. It leaned against the wire frame. I split the bolt into twenty-five shakes, packed them together and wired each end tight. I made up eight bundles to load on Jimmy.

Dad brought Jimmy and Betty up, and we loaded Jimmy. "Dad, you ride Betty and lead Jimmy and I'll walk along behind. Maybe I'll see some wildflowers."

As we started across the rocky manzanita flat, off to one side of the trail I spotted a tall-stemmed plant with a beautiful cluster of white, star-shaped flowers. I knew it grew on high rocky ridges, but never expected to find it out here on this rocky flat. Goodness knows, it was rocky enough for it.

This plant has an odd name, Zygadene, and it belongs to the lily family. Here in this dry rocky environment, it grows only about twenty inches tall. Some places it has been known to grow four feet tall.

The load of shakes rocked along with the shift of Jimmy's gait, so everything was fine. The high bank before the rocky ridge was ablaze with pink clarkia. Lizards were out on a high rock, looking over the situation. It's kind of comical to watch them raise themselves up on all four legs to their whole height of maybe half an inch, look all around, lower themselves, then repeat it. It was like they were doing push-ups.

Soon we arrived on the cabin flat.

"Where's a good place for the barn, Dad? We don't want to build too close to the creek: it'll be too cold in wintertime."

Dad walked over to a level spot about halfway down the flat and just below the trail, and said, "How about right here?"

"That looks good, Dad, and it's not too far from the creek. Later we can build a pole corral and extend it into the creek, so the animals can help themselves to water when they want it."

Dad led Jimmy over to the flat place and relieved him of his burden. "I'll take care of Jimmy and Betty, if you want to go get lunch, Leona."

"Okay. Leave the saddle on Jimmy and after lunch I'll ride up to the pack station."

At the cabin, I stirred the coals in the stove and made a pot of coffee. I opened a jar of apricots, and with some leftover biscuits from breakfast, we enjoyed a good lunch. When I was ready to start my afternoon ride, Dad said, "I'm going to work in the garden a while, then I'll sit down and sharpen my hoe." Dad took good care of his tools.

Of course, Happy was glad to be on the go again. My ride was quiet. It was too early in the day to see any deer, though I did flush out a couple of grouse as I rode through thick cedars on the east side of the mountain.

I picked up the roll of sacks and tied them on behind the saddle. The scythe was an awkward thing to carry. I wrapped the blade in several thicknesses of sacks so it wouldn't be so dangerous.

That evening Dad said, "Gee, we'll have to get the hay cut, stacked, cured and dried, then packed in here to the flat and stacked again before we know how big to build the barn."

"That's right. I want to build the barn over the hay. I don't see any sense in forking the hay over again to put it inside."

Next morning I put up a good lunch, and we rode out to cut hay, Dad with a pitchfork and I with the scythe. We looked dangerous, but there was no one to see us. I also had a good flat file to keep the scythe blade sharp. That's half the battle when you cut grass with a scythe.

We staked our horses and I started cutting grass. It was awkward at first, but after half an hour I found a good rhythm. The secret to using a scythe is not to grip the handles too tightly. Keep the heel of the blade on the ground and the point up an inch or so, and take a short step with each swing. By swinging your body rather than just your arms, you make better headway. I was cutting a swath about eight feet wide in a half moon shape described by the swing of my arms and body. I started the swing around to my right, turning left. At the end of the swing, I took a short step forward and started again on my right side. This left a nice windrow of hay behind me. As I looked back on it, I was right proud of it and thought of the peasant women I'd read about and seen pictures of scything hay. So it's true: it can be done.

By keeping the heel of the blade on the ground and the point low, oats are cut close to the ground. The grain was stiff and stood tall, which made cutting easier. The point of the scythe ran along under the mat of clover, so the stems cut cleanly and I wasn't pulling the blade through a mass of vine.

I didn't work long, for I didn't want my muscles too sore the first day. Still, we were well pleased with the day's work. We repeated this every day for a week, by which time Dad had a good many small shocks of hay curing.

At the end of the second week, we tried out the packing. With our hands, we gathered the hay from the shocks, stuffed it into the sacks and loaded one sack on each side of Jimmy and one on top, then did the same with Betty. It surprised us how much hay we loaded onto the animals.

By the time we had all the hay in and stacked, I figured I had to build a barn sixteen feet deep and fourteen feet wide. One reason for the depth was that the horse stalls faced the stacked hay across a low wall with mangers in between. Fourteen feet allowed plenty of width for the two horses as well as an eight- by six-foot saddle room with space enough for a sack or two of grain.

That evening, I sat at the table and figured how many boards I would need for the walls and how many shakes for the roof. The total came to 200 three-foot boards and 30 bundles of shakes. I probably figured more shakes than I actually needed. This would have cost around $300, which shows why it's important for a homesteader to have timber on his land. Moreover, this didn't include all the poles for the frame. That would be a big expense too, if I had to buy two by fours.

Dad helped me cut the poles and rafters for the barn. I put them up and nailed the boards on the walls, just as I had on the new room. I built a one-slope roof, sometimes called a shed-type building. It did away with the carpentry work of fitting rafters and filling in the A-shaped gable ends. A much simpler building to put together. We had a good place for the saddles and bridles and a few extra sacks of barley.

It felt good to know that the animals had refuge from heavy winter rainstorms. Things certainly looked better for the coming rainy season than it had one year before.

Later on, Dad helped me build the pole corral to take in a little of the creek. Then Jimmy and Betty were free to water themselves.

CHAPTER 20

WILD RASPBERRIES

On a calm day in early summer I saddled Jimmy and led him over to the garden where Dad was tending vegetables. The garden looked so nice and was really paying off. "I'm going over the mountain, down across Danfield Creek," I said, "and ride up on Oak Mountain a ways."

"Don't stay out too long. I get nervous if you don't come back in a reasonable time. I worry that maybe something happened."

"Oh Dad, don't go borrowing trouble."

"I know you're careful, and I shouldn't worry." He paused in thought. "I'm going to clean out a few weeds. The garden is doing so well, I certainly hope the deer don't find it."

"Don't work too long, Dad."

"No, I'll just sit down and sharpen my cross-cut saw."

"Okay, see you later."

When I rode across the rocky ridge I saw my little friends, the lizards, on a flat rock doing push-ups. On the rocky flat, a covey of mountain quail scurried under the heavy brush. I didn't stop to shoot any; they might be nesting around there somewhere.

Jimmy and I just poked along. When we reached Danfield Creek, he waded the stream and stopped for a drink, then climbed the bank where a lot of dogwood trees grew along the little flat that followed the creek bank. I jumped off Jimmy to look for a small dogwood to take back to the cabin, but never found it. I did find some limbs that drooped down almost to the ground. I took one and bent it about a foot from the tip until it broke on one side. I laid the limb on the moist soft earth, buried the break and placed a heavy rock on it to hold it there.

Next spring or sometime in the late winter, I thought I'd find my dogwood had rooted and then I could dig it up and transplant it in the yard close to the cabin. It's such a pretty tree with its profusion of big white blossoms.

I untied Jimmy, swung up into the saddle and started on my way again. Happy was glad to be on the move. The oaks and dogwood gave way to fir timber. I followed a well-defined deer trail that curved around the mountain until it opened into a burned out area, about an acre in size. I thought it might have been caused by a lighting strike. It was overgrown with wild raspberries—big, dark, purple, and ripe.

I jumped off Jimmy, tied him to a bush and started to eat berries. Gosh they were good! I didn't have a thing to collect some in. I hadn't even worn a hat.

I ate until I couldn't eat any more. Even Happy was picking them off the low runners and eating them. "Why don't we have something to carry a few berries back home?" I asked Happy. "We'll just have to go back to the cabin and come here again." That seemed fine to Happy, so I took Jimmy's bridle reins, tossed them up over his funny long ears and mounted. He was pleased to go home; he missed his beloved Betty.

I arrived at the cabin so soon, Dad wanted to know what was the matter. "Nothing," I said, "only you should see the big raspberry patch I found. The bushes are loaded with big ripe berries."

"My land, why don't we ride over there and pick a lot? Can you make jelly or jam out of them?"

"Sure can, Dad, and I just brought those dishes down from the pack station. There were a lot of mason jars and glasses in that tub. We have plenty of sugar on hand, too."

"Say, wouldn't that berry jelly go good on those hot biscuits you make, and on hotcakes?"

"Can't think of anything better, except for wild honey. Dad, let's get Walter to rob a beehive this fall. Then we'll have honey along with raspberry jelly all winter. Remember the swarms of bees on the goldenrod blossoms over at the ranch?"

Walter used to put flour on the bees, then time them to see how long it took to fly to their hive and back. He said that gave him an idea how far it was to the honey tree, and he watched where they flew. I guess it worked; he always found their hive.

That evening I washed the jars and glasses so they would be ready to fill. Next morning, we saddled up, carried four buckets over to the raspberry patch, tied our horses and started to pick berries. At first we put more in our stomachs than in the buckets, but we finally had them full.

The buckets went into sacks, one on each side of the saddle horn. The buckets couldn't be too full, or the motion of the horse would cause the berries to spill out into the sack, where they'd be mashed.

Back at the cabin, I fixed some lunch, then started on the berries. In the bottom of the buckets, there was quite a lot of juice, which I poured off for jelly. I heated up the berries and poured off more juice. I made jelly the old-fashioned way, measuring a cup of juice to a cup of sugar. I boiled the mixture down until it hung in a sheet from the edge of a spoon. Then it was ready to pour into glasses.

For jam, I poured a little less sugar into the berries and cooked them down. Raspberry jam has a lot of seeds in it unless it's run through a colander, which I didn't have, so the seeds stayed in. That was all right. Dad was fortunate enough to still have his own teeth and, of course, I did too. (People with a plate or false teeth have a problem with the seeds.)

Every jar and glass was full! We would have plenty to last us all next winter. That evening, Dad looked at all the jam and jelly and said, "By Golly! That was a good trip to get all those berries."

We were also fortunate that the old Smith orchard was

accessible. This land had been taken up by a homesteader, who planted about twenty acres during the 1880s. Now some of the trees were dead and gone. Smith had not proved up on it, and the land reverted back to the Government. In 1918, Gilbert Smith, no relation, filed on it and proved up on it. Then the rancher who owned 5,000 acres around it bought him out. He didn't do anything with the orchard; his house was miles away from it. We picked pears, plums, apples, and cherries for canning. The peach trees were all gone but almond trees and English walnuts survived, though it was hard to get any nuts, because the gray squirrels ate them before they were ripe.

I used to ride up there sometimes just to sit in the grass and watch the animals come in to feed on the fallen fruit. There would be does, fawns, bucks, wild hogs, pigs, rabbits, quail and grouse, though, of course, they were not there all together. Usually when hogs were there, no other animals came.

The large open ridges were covered with high wild grass and in the afternoon a gentle breeze blew in from the coast, and I would imagine it was an ocean wave rolling across the hillside. When it crested the top of the ridge, it broke and started all over again at the bottom.

Sometimes I would hear a band of little pigs coming along in single file, each one grunting in a low monotonous tone, "oink, oink oink," like they were talking to one another. Their hair was so covered in tarweed, it stuck straight out from their little round bodies like pincushions. If they didn't see or smell me, they'd just go on grunting, oinking their way around the hill, but oh my, if they saw me they scattered and hid like a bunch of newly hatched quail.

When I was out this way and I used my eyes to see and my ears to hear, I was part of God's great creation. It gave me such a feeling of security and peacefulness. I guess that's one reason I never felt lonely.

CHAPTER 21

RATTLESNAKES

I've never had a great love for rattlesnakes. I've killed many. In fact, I killed my first when I was only nine years old. One evening, after tramping down in the pasture to fetch the cows, I came across a rattler that disputed the trail with me. He lay coiled in the trail and was not about to let me pass. I carried a .22 and immediately shot him.

The .22 was made by Winchester in 1903 and was a neat little automatic. The rifle held ten cartridges in the magazine, which was in the stock. You pulled the magazine spring part way out of the back end of the stock and loaded the small shells in a slot in the center of the stock, then closed it by pushing the magazine rod and spring back in. Winchester discontinued manufacturing this neat little rifle years ago.

Several times rattlesnakes have struck at me, barely missing their mark, but I've never been bitten. My sister and I had a scary horseback ride one day when we were quite young. We had ridden down the county road between high grassy banks. One particular stretch was quite level. Winona and I lifted the reins on the horses' necks and they broke into an easy rocking-chair lope. All of a sudden I saw something out of the corner of my eye go hurtling across our backs, right over the rumps of both horses just behind the cantle of our saddles.

I screamed at Winona, "Did you see that?"

"Yes! A huge rattlesnake struck at us."

"Let's go back and see if we can find him!" We pulled up

our horses, whirled around, galloped back and came to a sliding halt. I jumped off, pulled my rifle out of the scabbard and loaded it. "You'd better hold my horse's reins."

"I hear him," Winona said. "Do you?"

"I think he's under that big manzanita bush below the road. I'll go down the bank a step or two and see if I can spy him." I could hear rattles going, buzzing like mad.

"Don't get close to him!" Winona yelled.

I spied him against the trunk of the manzanita, worked around a little, took good aim at his head and fired.

"Did you get him?" Winona called.

"Yeah. He's big, too. I bet he's three-and-a-half feet or more, with big, long rattles." I climbed up on the road, shoved my rifle back in the scabbard and swung up into the saddle. "Gee! How could we be so lucky that he didn't strike one of the horses, or one of us? He never hit the road; he landed over the bank. I bet he was blind and struck when he felt the vibration of the ground from the horses' feet."

"We don't need anything like that again," Winona said.

This brings to mind a near tragedy at the homestead in early fall. Winona and her husband, Elbert, had come up to the cabin to visit us, and Elbert wanted to get some small pigs. Winona, Elbert and I trekked out one evening to the tall oats on the west side of Fir Mountain. I was ahead on Jimmy, Elbert walked behind Jimmy with Happy following, and Winona was a little farther back. It wasn't long before Happy smelled some pigs and took off. She bayed a bunch of little pigs against an old fir log.

"Come on!" Elbert hollered. "Jump off your horses and let's catch some pigs."

We did well, catching three pigs. I took the roll of grain sacks off Jimmy's saddle and we put a pig apiece in a grain sack and tied them on Betty.

"That's enough pigs," Elbert said. "Let's go back to the cabin."

"Don't you want to ride a ways?" I asked.

"No, I'll walk."

rattlesnake

We started back towards the cabin with two pigs on Betty with Winona and one on Jimmy with me and had almost reached the fir timber when we noticed that Happy was gone again. We stopped and listened and pretty soon heard her baying. Elbert ran around the hill to her and we heard him shoot. Winona and I followed to where Elbert had shot a nice big black hog. After Elbert dressed it out, we loaded it on Jimmy. I took his reins and continued on foot as we headed again for home.

When we hit the top of the mountain, we stopped to catch our breath. Winona said, in a worried tone, "Leona, where's Happy?"

"Isn't she here?"

"Listen," said Elbert. "I don't hear her barking."

"You know," Winona said, "When we were going down the other side of the mountain in those tall oats, I saw her jump sideways and she let out a little yip."

"I bet a snake struck her," Elbert said. "You girls wait here. I'll go back and see if I can find her."

Thirty minutes later, Elbert came back carrying Happy in his arms. "That snake did get her, I guess. When I spotted her, she was moving slow and whimpering. When she saw me, she just stopped and waited for me to get to her. She looked up at me with big brown eyes that said, 'I hurt. Please pick me up.'"

"Elbert," Winona said, "hand me your rifle. I'll carry it if you're going to carry Happy."

Before long we arrived at the cabin. Elbert took Happy inside and laid her on the rug in the living room. "I'll go help Dad hang up the hog, and take care of the little ones. You girls see what's the matter with Happy."

Winona and I examined Happy and, sure enough, the rattler had struck her left hind foot. Winona fixed supper while I spent all my time with Happy. It didn't seem like I could do much. I soaked her foot in a basin of warm Lysol water, but I don't know if that did any good. She kept whimpering and seemed to want me to stay with her. I sat up with her all night.

By the next morning her whole left side was badly swollen clear to the end of her nose. She wouldn't eat anything, although she did drink a lot of water.

Elbert meanwhile had built a little pigpen in the corner of the saddle room, laid down a lot of hay and turned the little pigs in there. Next day he put the little pigs in sacks, because he and Winona were getting ready to go home. I told them to take the big hog, too, for I could get another one. Elbert packed the hog and pigs on Jimmy. Winona rode Betty while Elbert and I plodded on foot up to the car. After seeing them off, I returned to the cabin to tend to Happy.

After the fourth or fifth day, Happy began to eat a little. Her swelling was going down, and she moved around more easily. She continued to improve slowly. It took her about six weeks to fully recover. I was so glad when she was her old self again. She was such good company as well as a valuable dog. How would I ever catch hogs if I didn't have her?

Those darn snakes! They always pop up where you least expect them.

One day I was ready to tie Jimmy up and do a little fishing. I led him over to an oak tree and glancing down, well, gosh-darn if I didn't see a rattlesnake only a foot from my foot! His head was sticking out of a hole in the base of the tree. He dodged back in the hole where I couldn't see him. I didn't lose much time finding another tree to tie Jimmy to. I unsaddled Jimmy and threw one of his saddle blankets over the snake hole, then went on about my fishing.

When I came back two hours later, I fetched my Winchester and marched over to the hole and jerked the blanket off. Mr. Rattlesnake was right there, staring at me. I popped him in the head with a bullet.

I've done this many times. It's a creepy feeling to climb around a bank along the creek and see a rattlesnake looking you in the eye from a hole in the bank.

Over at the Las Lomas Ranch we had a little saddle horse named Peanuts. If you were out fishing and came up to her when she wasn't tied and started pulling the line out fast from the clicking reel, she was gone like a streak of lightning and you had to hoof it home. She thought the clicking reel was the sound of a rattlesnake's rattle! Betty was afraid of rattlers, too. Jimmy wasn't. I've seen him walk right over them as if he couldn't care less. I never understood why they didn't strike him.

I know of several people who have been bitten by snakes. They usually stay in the hospital a week, but it takes quite a while to get over a rattlesnake strike. Nearly all the stricken dogs I have seen swelled terribly, but most of them survived. I think a lot depends on the amount of venom the snake has. If it had used the venom recently, it would take some time to build up a lethal dose.

CHAPTER 22

THE NEW TRAIL

It was fall now, the leaves of the oak trees had turned a golden yellow and some were blowing off, anticipating winter. The evenings were cool, and a small fire blazed in old Hazel. I sat in front of the stove and said, "Dad, I've been wondering if it would be possible to go around the north side of the mountain to the pack station."

"It could be. Maybe we ought to try it."

"It's such a long haul to climb the mountain, only to have to go down again to the low divide where the pack station is. Would you walk around there with me tomorrow? I don't think we'd ever get through with the horse and mule."

"I've kind of wondered if there wasn't a better way in here. Sure, I'll go."

"We'd better take our axes; we don't know what we might find."

"Let's go in the morning, say about nine o'clock. Is that okay?"

"Yes, I'll fix a couple of sandwiches. Maybe we'd better take a canteen of water. I haven't found many springs on the north side of a mountain, and we know there's no water near the pack station."

Next morning, Dad fed Jimmy and Betty some hay and barley, while I baked a pan of biscuits for breakfast.

"Well, they're fed," he said, "and they can water themselves. You know, the corral is working out great. I bet they like it, too."

"Too bad we can't take 'em with us, but we might find some terrible rough country in there."

We ate a good breakfast, then I cleaned up the cabin, Dad picked up the axes, I made lunch, and at last we were ready.

When I popped out the door, Happy greeted me, laughing and showing her teeth. Her name suited her well. She slept down in the barn now, on some hay in the saddle room. I think she liked the company of Betty and Jimmy. It was so nice to have this barn for the animals.

Dad glanced at his watch, a beautiful old gold timepiece in a closed case. He'd had it for forty years or more, he told me, and the gold case was worn thin. That watch was his pride and joy. The day the Las Lomas house burned, he had it in the pocket of his blue bib overalls. I wasn't so lucky; I had a nice engraved gold watch that had belonged to Mother, but unfortunately I wasn't wearing it that day. Walter, Dad and I were out building a new picket fence in one of the pastures that had been burned out by a forest fire the summer before. All we had left after the fire were the clothes on our backs.

It was just nine in the morning when Dad and I started out. We followed the trail where it turned up the mountain and wound around onto the Cedar Creek side of the mountain through heavy brush and thick little cedar trees. We chopped our way through and then came into big fir trees spaced about thirty feet apart. The side hill was not very steep, so it was pretty good walking. Gray squirrels ran up and down the firs. They'd sit on a limb and scold us, probably for encroaching on their territory. We blazed some trees as we walked along.

The trail we were blazing was about three hundred feet above Cedar Creek, but there was too much timber for us to be able to see the creek. As we trudged on, the trail opened up and now we could see across the canyon where deer were feeding on manzanita brush—nice and sunny on that side.

It was pretty country and it greeted us with changing prospects. Here was a big manzanita thicket. The brush had been broken by a heavy snowstorm at some earlier date and it was one big mess. We started to chop our way through huge bushes lying criss-cross in a tangled mess. Most of them were still alive.

"Dad, we'll never get through this today. I think we'd better blaze our way as we climb over it and get around to the pack station. Maybe this isn't so good after all."

"Guess you're right. We'd better get through before we try to chop and clear a way to walk."

We finally made our way out of the manzanita thicket and found the going good. We were in big pepperwoods for a while, then fine loose shale rock. The grade was level; we stayed about the same distance above the creek all the way. We saw more deer on the other side of the creek.

"This would make a great trail to hunt from, Dad."

"Yes, I like the looks of it; so far it's a wonderful grade."

"It mustn't be too far around to the pack station. Looks to me like the manzanita patch is the hardest thing to get through."

We soon came out at the pack station and sat down to rest. We had followed the gradual rise of the creek all the way around the mountain. I could see Dad was tired, so I said, "We'd better take the trail over the mountain going back; that manzanita thicket is too hard to get through."

We rested, ate our sandwiches and drank some water. It was now past noon. "Whenever you're ready, we'll start for home," I said.

"Oh, I'm ready any time."

We took our time walking back to the cabin. Betty whinnied to Dad when we arrived down in the flat. Jimmy never had anything to say, except when he called to Betty. Dad stopped to feed Jimmy and Betty a little more hay and give them their grain. Once in the cabin, I started a fire in the cook stove. I knew Dad was hungry.

That evening all we could talk about was the new trail. It would be a great improvement over the mountain trail, but it meant a lot of work. I suggested we wait until a good rain, so we wouldn't have dust to contend with.

"I think that's a good idea," Dad said. "In fact, it's a job we can work on all winter when it's not raining."

"We only have to work on it when we feel like it," I said. "Won't it be great when we're able to go up to the pack station and the end of the road without climbing that mountain every time?"

First there was a mile of trail to build, but we were both thrilled over the prospect of a new trail over such a nice even grade on a good side hill. The soil was loose and there probably would only be about an eight- to twelve-inch bank to grade out a trail twenty or thirty inches wide with, apparently, no hard rock to go through.

CHAPTER 23

MY GOOD FRIENDS

Irving and Beulah Berry were good friends. Irving was on the Santa Rosa police force and loved his rifles and pistol. Beulah was a school superintendent at the Monroe School outside Santa Rosa. They had good jobs during the Depression and were a big help to us.

For several years they'd hunted deer and wild hogs at Las Lomas Ranch. When Irving had his vacation in July or August, they always asked me to go with them on a three-week camping trip. Lucky me. We traveled through every county north of San Francisco, mostly in a five-passenger Model A Ford. We never took a tent. Slept on army folding cots. I remember some terrible thunder, lightning and rain storms. One storm drove us to a motor court for the night.

What fun we had fishing for trout and watching deer, sometimes seeing as many as three big mule deer feeding in a green meadow among the tall Ponderosa Pines in the high Sierra.

Deer hunting season came later. Walter and Irving went back to that beautiful country and found their big mule bucks. I don't think they ever failed to get a buck apiece.

After the Las Lomas Ranch was gone,they asked if they could come to the homestead. "Of course," I answered. "Why not? We still have deer and wild hogs to hunt, and also trout fishing."

Beulah was a good cook and Irving was a good worker out on the trails, where he helped us cut and trim brush. They always brought lots of ammunition for the rifles and pistols, including my own. Once, Walter, Irv, Beulah and I were working up on the mountain cutting brush when we ran out of drinking water.

"I'll take the canteen and slide down through the brush to Cedar Creek and fill it," Walter said.

Irv said, "Walt, better take my .38 revolver. You don't know what you might run into down there, maybe an old boar hog or mountain lion."

"Oh, it's not likely."

Nevertheless, Irv unbuckled his belt and handed it and his revolver over to Walter, who buckled it on and took off. Beulah, Irv, and I kept on working. Time ticked by and we were about famished for water. Finally Irv said, "What in the world is taking Walt so long? He's been gone an hour and a half."

When he showed up, all he had to say was, "Gee it's a long way down there! The brush was so thick I had a hard time getting through. It was ten times worse climbing back up. I would've done better to go back to the cabin for the water."

A long time later, I found out that Walter had lost Irv's revolver and it took him all that time to find it. In fact, he was lucky to ever find it.

The months flew by. It was the day before Thanksgiving when in burst Irving and Beulah. After greetings and some visiting, Irving said, "Leona, there are a lot of groceries up in the car. Do you want Beulah and me to take Jimmy and Betty and go back for them?"

"No, why don't you stay here and visit with Dad, and Beulah and I will go get them. Is that all right with you, Beulah?"

"Sure."

I saddled up the animals and Beulah and I took off for the car. On the side of the mountain we flushed out a couple of coveys of mountain quail. They are big, with orange, reddish brown and gold coloring in their breast feathers, beautiful birds. They don't fly much but they love to run along under the manzanita brush up the slope of the mountain.

When we arrived at the car I looked in and said, "My land, you must have bought out the store!" In with the groceries was a large turkey, canned cranberries, and all the fixings. I packed the groceries into four grain sacks and hung one on each side of the saddle horns, so Beulah and I could ride back to the cabin.

We carried the groceries into the cabin while Dad took Jimmy and Betty down to the barn. It was nice to be able to say, "Dad took the animals to the barn," now that we had a real farm. We spent that evening telling stories. We were always glad to see Irving and Beulah.

The next morning, after a hearty breakfast of bacon and eggs, toast and plenty of raspberry jam, Beulah and I tackled the turkey. She made the dressing and stuffed the turkey; I baked pumpkin pies. Now came the time to put the turkey in the oven. When Beulah shoved the pan in, it went in only halfway.

"Leona, what are we going to do? The turkey's too big for the oven! I can't shut the door!"

"Oh, I'll fix that. I'll prop a board in front of the opening and put in more of Dad's dry manzanita wood. We can turn the bird around every once in a while and I bet that old bird will cook."

Sure enough, it took about thirty minutes longer than it would have if the door had been shut, but it came out cooked to perfection—a beautiful golden brown. We had mashed potatoes, sweet potatoes and lots of good old golden brown gravy to go with everything.

What a memorable dinner! I was thankful for a great many things: good friends, always plenty to eat, a comfortable cabin, and the fact that the Depression wasn't bothering Dad and me. I was enjoying every minute. I had so much time to visit the great outdoors, and to think that all I could see and all I could hear was mine to enjoy. It was God's great gift to one and all.

We all went to bed that night feeling very thankful.

When the sun peeked over the mountain at the head of the canyon, I sensed it would be a warm fall day. About ten-thirty in the morning, Dad was out by the garden trimming out a tree he wanted to cut for wood, and Beulah and I were in the backyard when Irv walked past us, headed toward the front of the cabin. At the open dining room window, the sun was shining halfway across the floor. "Leona," Irv hollered, "there's a big mountain lizard in the middle of the living room floor!"

"I dare you to shoot him!" I yelled.

We heard a loud bang. Irv had shot it with his .38 revolver.

"I didn't think you would do that," I said.

"Well, you better not dare me to do something."

We all had a big laugh over it, then I had to tell a story on myself:

"Last winter, Dad and I were sitting in front of the fire one evening. I had the Aladdin lamp lit so the room was nice and bright. Well, a big old woodrat came across the ceiling log between the living room and kitchen and stopped in the corner. That was his mistake. I reached for my rifle and shot him. Oh well, another hole or two didn't hurt the cabin; it just made for a little better ventilation."

We all had another good laugh. Yes, we were happy. We were never sick; we didn't even have colds. But that weekend was one I'll never forget. "Leona," Irving said, "we hunt and fish up here all the time and enjoy so many weekends, we'd like to give you something."

"Oh", I said, "You do a lot of work here and help us in other ways."

"No, that's not enough," Irv said.

"Well, all right, if you feel that way." I had no idea that what they had in mind was a 1925 Chevrolet car! Irving drove it up the next weekend and Beulah drove their car up so they could drive home. That car changed my life around, and would remain with me for the next fifteen years. I did every-

Model made of the homestead cabin by Leona Cox.
— *Photo by David Giles*

thing under the sun with its help. I could write a book about it, but, piffle, it would make this story never end.

CHAPTER 24

THE LITTLE CHEVY
THAT COULD

The little Chevy opened up a whole new life for me. The next time I went to Santa Rosa, I bought a second-hand car battery, and I used it with the Atwater-Kent radio, replacing the drycells. When I traveled to Santa Rosa, about once every six weeks, I packed the radio battery up to the car on Jimmy and after I traveled a ways I stopped and switched batteries. By the time I drove to Santa Rosa and back it was fully charged, good for another six weeks on the radio.

We now used the radio about an hour a day, mostly for news. I was able to increase my meager supply of money, too. A few days before I planned to go to town, Happy and I went hog hunting, and we usually got two hogs. I took good care of the meat and, just before I was ready to go, I cut and wrapped

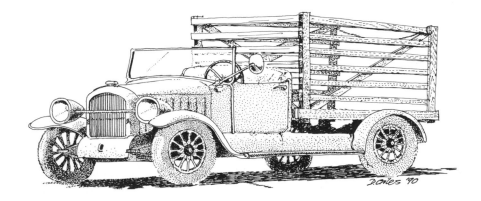

packages of chops, roasts, ham roasts and picnic hams. I weighed each package and wrote the price on it. Soon I had standing orders from people in Santa Rosa.

When I arrived in Santa Rosa, the first thing I did was deliver the meat and collect money for it—more than enough to buy groceries and gasoline. The little Chevy was easy on gas. I actually started saving money.

I stayed two nights in town, sometimes with Walter and Maude, other times with Beulah and Irving. Dad knew I would be back the third day so he was always at the pack station waiting for me. Happy jumped around when she saw me and ran up the road to greet me. Dad wanted to know how the trip went and if I sold the meat all right.

"The meat always goes, Dad; I probably could sell more."

In the wintertime I parked the little Chevy on top of the first terrible steep grade. It would sit out there through the storms, wind, rain and snow. I always kept a five gallon bucket in the car and, during the winter months when I left it, I drained the water out of the radiator and engine block into the bucket.

When I returned in six weeks, I shut the petcock on the radiator and engine block, poured the water back into the radiator, climbed in, pulled the choke cable out a little and stepped on the starter. It started right up, just purred like a kitten.

That reminds me that somebody gave me two gray kittens that looked just alike. I didn't know what to name them and I couldn't tell them apart, so I called one Puss and the other one Puss- puss. I had them for a long time.

In the spring, Walter spent a weekend with us and we graded the road with a small vee grader that I made. I always graded downhill, then loaded the vee on the back of the little Chevy and hauled it back up the hill. I cut the body of the car off just behind the front seat and made a flat bed-truck that way. Later I built racks to install in the truck bed so I could haul lambs and ewes, fence posts, woven wire, hay and grain. The Chevy was small, but very mighty. Later on, I cut cords of four-foot wood into stove-wood lengths or chunk heater wood by jacking up one rear wheel and running a long canvas belt over the wheel and back over the pulley on the mandrel of a circle saw blade. The Chevy also pumped water for one of the neighbors when his pump broke down.

I pulled a two-horse mower with it and mowed a lot of hay, and I also pulled a big hay rake to rake the hay into windrows. It was really a workhorse. I used it as one would use a small tractor. It never was in a garage. The winter rain and frost action on the inside banks of the road loosens the dirt, and even the rock, if it is a little on the shale side. The vee grader picked that up and slid it across the ruts and holes to smooth the road, besides widening it a few inches a year. It was a great help to me.

The little Chevy stayed with me for fifteen years. What a marvelous gift!

CHAPTER 25

TROUT AND EAGLES

Dad was working in his garden one late spring when I went down to talk to him. "Dad, it's such a great day, I'm going to saddle Jimmy and ride to the low divide, then go down to Cedar Creek and catch a mess of trout. We haven't had any for quite a while."

"Say, wouldn't it be nice to have a pan of fried trout and a big bowl of French-fried potatoes for dinner tonight?"

"That's the way I feel, and I'm going to do something about it."

Down at the barn I grabbed the manure fork and dug some angle worms, plopped them in the Prince Albert tobacco can I kept in the saddle room, and slipped them into my shirt pocket. I saddled Jimmy and led him up to the cabin and tied him. I made myself a sandwich and rolled it up with a flour sack and a grain sack, grabbed my fishing rod and rifle and tied everything on the saddle. "I'll be gone until sometime this afternoon, I imagine."

"Don't be too late and do be careful."

"Okay, see you later."

I put my foot in the stirrup and swung up into the saddle. It was fun to ride Jimmy. He was a willing little traveler and you never really knew what he was going to do next. He never bucked with the saddle on, but he didn't want to be ridden bareback, for some reason. He didn't find anything to be afraid of this morning, so the ride was peaceful.

I spied some gray squirrels as I rode through the big firs

on the mountain. I was riding along a pretty sidehill of scattered oaks and green grass, where quite a few deer were feeding. They went bouncing away like they had springs in their legs—such graceful animals. The fawns were losing their spotted coats. They soon would be taller and all brown, with a little white on their briskets and the inside of their legs. The undersides of their tails were white and, when they trotted away from you, their tails always stood straight up like white flags.

I was following a well-defined trail and, of all things, came upon a picket fence with a small picket gate. It was shut so I got off, opened it and led Jimmy through. We were on the creek now, so I tied Jimmy to a tree, grabbed my fishing rod and said to Happy, "You stay here with Jimmy and don't let any thing happen to him. I don't want to walk home."

I rigged up my rod, tied on a small hook and threaded a worm onto it. I dropped it into the first good hole I came to. It wasn't any time until a nice trout was dangling on my line. I

found a green pepperwood switch and had something to
string my trout on.

I fished down the creek a ways. It was pretty, with big
rocks out in the middle and the banks all covered with moss.
There were big pools of water with small waterfalls and usually a nice trout lurking somewhere in back of the waterfall
waiting to grab the worm as it eddied in behind the waterfall.
It was exciting. One never knew when a big trout would hit
the hook.

Tiger lilies were in bloom along the bank. Occasionally, a
clump stuck out in the middle of the stream where a bunch of
rocks made a little island. Their stems stood tall among the
grass and ferns, with beautiful orange blossoms speckled
with brown. All along the banks were fawn lilies, their large
flat green leaves marked with white splotches like little
fawns. The blossoms were all gone.

It didn't take long to fill my switch with nice trout, so I
turned and picked my way back up the creek, stopping here
and there to admire the large five-fingered ferns that grew
along the overhanging banks. I could have caught more trout,
but I had all I needed to cook a nice meal.

I walked up to Jimmy. Happy was glad to see me and
jumped all over me as much as to say, "I'm so glad you came
back." I untied Jimmy and we walked back through the little
gate and out into the sunshine. There was nice grass here, so I
staked Jimmy out on my long lasso rope and pulled his bridle
off so he could graze. I took the rolled-up sack off the saddle,
found a good place to sit and ate lunch, sharing it with
Happy. We had sandwiches, jerky, dried prunes and a walnut
or two. Happy liked whatever she could get from me.

After lunch, I wrapped the fish in green grass and rolled
them in the flour sack and then in the grain sack. They would
stay nice and cold until I reached the cabin.

I put Jimmy's bridle on, coiled up my lariat and tied it on
the saddlehorn. We were ready to go home. We took our time
climbing the mountain and rode over the top to the edge of

the rocky flat and the head of the little canyon where I'd killed two bucks the first day I came into this country.

I saw a golden eagle swoop down and go out of sight for a few seconds. I kicked Jimmy in the ribs and we galloped over just as the eagle came back in sight, so close to me I saw he was having trouble rising. He had a small kid goat in his talons. When he saw me he dropped the kid. I jumped off Jimmy, jerked the reins over his head and ran down to the little kid. Jimmy was no problem: he ran with me just like a dog on a leash.

I picked the little goat up in my arms and cuddled him. He was alive but soon quit breathing. When I examined him, the eagle's claws had penetrated both sides of his little chest, probably puncturing both lungs. It made me sad to think such a young animal had to die. I carried him over to a manzanita bush, tied Jimmy to a limb, then laid the little kid down. With my pocket knife I dug a big hole, gently laid the kid in and covered him with dirt. Then I found a big rock to put on it so nothing would dig it up. I felt a little better, knowing I had done the best I could for him.

That evening I had plenty to tell Dad. Every day brought another adventure, sometimes good and sometimes rather sad. Isn't that true throughout life, though?

CHAPTER 26

ONE MORE ROOM

I decided to add on another bedroom for company, extended out from the kitchen. What had been the back door would now go into the bedroom, and a door in the east end of the new room would lead outside. It would be built the same as the other rooms. What might cause problems, I thought, was getting a double bedspring down from the pack station.

One day up there I looked at the mesh spring with a wood frame. The corners were bolted together, but I could take the bolts out and roll it bottom to top and tie it up.

Dad helped me make the boards and shakes to build the room. We cut poles for the studs and got them down to the cabin and Betty dragged the material over to the site. After I had the frame up and closed in, Dad helped wheel the dirt over to make the floor. It was finished off with hard packed shale rock just like the other floor. I peeled poles and made a double bedstead for the north side of the room. On the south side I built in two bunks, a lower and an upper.

Now I was ready to get the spring. Dad rode up with me. I carried a wrench to take the spring apart. We laid the side rails across the spring, then rolled it up and fastened it with baling wire. We split a small bale of hay for the rolled-up bedspring on one side and mattress on the other. We tied them both down to the saddle cinch ring and were ready to head for the cabin. My worries were all for nothing.

I had mattresses and covers for the cots and threw down a couple of deer skins on the hard-packed shale rock for rugs in front of the bed and the lower bunk. When I built the walls, I framed in a small window on the north wall and one on the east end. I didn't have the windows to put in but figured to buy some first time I went to town. Maybe I could find some secondhand ones for little or nothing.

Later that fall we built a woodshed to the north of the back door. On the west end, I boarded up only the lower half of the wall and left a doorway open on the south wall corner. Air blew through, but very little rain drifted in. Dad helped me put a big strong pole across the top plate from wall to wall to hang hogs or deer out of the rain. Dad always kept lots of dry wood in the shed, and now we had a place to store our tools.

One day, I received a letter from the U.S. Government Land Office. They wanted some pictures of the land, especially the tree- covered hillsides. I borrowed a camera and sent them the pictures. Several months later, a Government inspector walked in to see the timber. He laughed when I showed him how tiny the trees were.

He said, "Why those trees would never grow big enough to cut for lumber in a million years." In fact, he didn't even know what the trees were.

I said, "They look like a juniper to me, but everybody around here calls them cedars. They're not cedar, at least not like any cedar I ever saw. "

"I'll take a limb back to the office," he said, "and find out what they are and let you know."

In due time a letter came. The trees were classed as a cross between cedar and hemlock. The "Fremontia Journal" of the California Native Plant Society classed them as Sargent Cypress. The article explained that they grow on a serpentine soil and that there are only a few in all the United States. This particular stand was one of the largest.

My claim was situated on the north edge of the stand. The Sargent Cypress extends as far south as Occidental in Sonoma County, California. There is a small stand of them northeast of Cloverdale, in Lake County, California.

Less unusual was our little outhouse. I built one east of the back, corner of the woodshed. It faced the rocky ridge just across the creek. This is the ridge we saw the first time we came over the mountaintop. I was sitting on the throne in the little lodge one morning as the sun slowly rose over the ridge and a great big buck walked out on a cliff shelf and stood there with the sun reflecting off his horns. What a picture he made!

I truly wished for a good camera. Winona, Mother and I had made a hobby of developing film and printing pictures when we lived over at Las Lomas. Mother had a wonderful Eastman folding camera that took postcard-size pictures. It was lost in the fire in 1926. What a loss! It took a long time to recover from that fire. Some keepsakes can never be replaced.

We were almost living in a normal way. We had a four-room house, a barn for the saddle stock, and a good wood-shed, with little invested except time. I enjoyed making the boards and shakes and cutting and trimming the poles for framework. The house had worked out so well it was a joy to be inside. Combined with the outdoor joys of riding, hunting and fishing trips—what more could one wish for?

CHAPTER 27

THE YOUNG LADIES

We had just finished our lunch when we heard Happy bark, then a knock on the cabin door. I looked out the window and couldn't see anything, but when I opened the door, to my great surprise, off to one side stood two young ladies. They were dressed in suits, skirts and trim jackets and, of all things, silk stockings and high heeled pumps.

Well, needless to say, I was dumbfounded. Finally I found my voice and said, "My goodness, are you lost?"

One said, "Heavens, I don't know, but I think we have found the end of the earth. We are looking for a person by the name of Charles Henry Dixon."

What have we done? I wondered. Are these ladies game wardens, deputy sheriffs or what?

"Yes, he lives here." I introduced myself and invited them in.

The lady who asked the question introduced herself. "I am Miss Davis, and this is Miss Standley. We have come from the Sonoma County Health and Welfare office to have Mr. Dixon fill out some papers. He then can draw his old age pension."

"Have you ladies had any lunch?" I asked as I introduced them to Dad.

"No," Miss Davis said.

"Then I'll fix some for you. Would you like a cup of coffee?"

"Oh, that would save my life, I think," Miss Davis said.

Miss Standley said, "I'm sure we will need something before we can make it back over that horrible mountain."

"How in the world did you ever walk in here in those high-heeled pumps?"

"I don't know," Miss Standley said, "and I've lost the heel off one of my shoes."

I gave them a good lunch and made fresh hot coffee. When they were finished they both thanked me. Miss Davis talked to Dad, and Miss Standley said to me, "If we'd had any idea it was such a trip in here we certainly would have dressed differently."

Miss Davis showed Dad a lot of papers and had him sign his name to them. She said, "When these papers are processed you will receive a check for $15 the first of every month."

Dad finally spoke. "I don't understand this. I've never signed up for relief in my life."

"Mr. Dixon, this isn't relief," Miss Davis said. "This is for everyone over 65 years of age. It's legitimate and is paid by the government and the county you live in. Besides, I think anyone living in a backwoods environment like this should be paid to do so."

"We're not on relief like so many people," I replied, "and we get by nicely. Besides, we enjoy living in this wild country, as you call it."

The ladies looked around the cabin and Miss Davis said, "You do have a nice cabin. It's small but you have it fixed so nice and pretty with papered walls and all. You should see some of the homestead cabins we've visited. I don't see how people can exist in them, let alone call them home."

Dad signed the papers rather reluctantly. The ladies visited a little more, then Miss Davis said, "We'd better get started back up that mountain. It's going to be a terrible hike."

"You ladies wait here and I'll go saddle the horses."

I marched down to the barn, saddled Betty and Jimmy, and led them up to the cabin. When the ladies came out, I asked, "Have you ever ridden a horse?"

They both answered, "Oh my, no!"

"Well, it's simple. Miss Davis, come over here and place your left foot in the stirrup. Now grab the horn with your hands and give yourself a slight push with your right foot and pull with your hands. Swing your right leg up and over the horse's rump. There you go! You're up in the saddle."

I turned to the other lady. "Now, Miss Standley, you have Jimmy and he's little and low. You won't have any problem. Do just as Miss Davis did. There you go, you made it! I'll hand you the reins."

"Oh, no! Please, just lead him. I'll feel much safer."

"All right. Are you ready?"

"I guess so." They waved goodbye to Dad.

We arrived at their car with no further problems, but when they dismounted they were both so stiff from their hike in, and the horseback ride back, that they could hardly stand up. Still, they thanked me for the ride, and Miss Davis said, "We'll come back next year to see how you're getting by. You do expect to be here?"

"Absolutely," I said. With that they got into their car and drove off. But they never did come back. The first of the month came and Dad received $15. It wasn't much, but it was a help. That evening, Dad said, "Leona, I feel kind of guilty taking that money."

"Dad, listen, you've lived in Sonoma County for over thirty years and paid out many dollars in taxes, so don't feel bad about it; just be grateful you have it coming."

"Yeah, I guess you're right. Might as well take it."

CHAPTER 28

TRAIL WORK

Thanksgiving over, there was now frost in the air in the early morning. We'd had a heavy downpour of rain, and water was splashing high in the little ravines and flowing down the hillsides, driven by heavy, sharp gusts of wind. The oaks were like black scarecrows, their fall dressing of golden leaves lay on the ground, soggy and wet. In the evening after we had finished our dinner and were sitting in front of the fire, I tried to find my way around on an old mandolin I'd bought the last time I was in town. I'd played one at the Las Lomas ranch, before the fire, and the old tunes revived my memory.

"Dad, why don't you play something? Did you ever play as a boy?"

He laughed. "No, I never had a chance to even try. My brother Will and I were always working. Besides, I couldn't carry a tune in a basket. I always enjoyed the music you and Winona played and the Red Seal records your Mother had on the Victrola."

"Me, too. We had some nice records." I liked to listen to Caruso, Harry Lauder, tenor John McCormack and Souza's Marches.

"Leona, if your mother could be with us, she'd thoroughly enjoy this life. She loved the hunting trips she took with Walter and you, the great trout fishing days when you three girls took a lunch and your rods and hiked down to Wild Cattle Creek and fished down to the county road. And I drove down in the spring wagon and picked you up at the bottom of the Las Lomas grade late in the afternoon. Those were the days."

"Yes, they were fine days, but let's get back on track here. How about going out on the trail in the morning with a few tools to look the situation over?"

"It would be a fine time to start. The dust has sure settled for the rest of this year."

"If we start on it now, we should be done by early spring. Wow! Wouldn't it be great to go to the pack station around the mountain instead of over it?"

"I'm ready," Dad answered.

The next morning was brisk and cool, a great day to work. We saddled Jimmy and Betty and gathered up a saw, two axes and a mattock and took off for the trail work.

"Let's come in by one o'clock, Dad. That will be enough work for the first day."

We rode out to the trees that Walter, Dean and I had tied our horses to the first day we came into this part of the country. The little cedars were so thick there was no way to get the horses through. We soon chopped our way in, however, and came into big scattered Douglas fir and pepperwoods. I could visualize the trail. It would be a pretty trail to ride.

Gray squirrels were already up, playing and chattering as they tore around through the trees. When they saw us, they rushed up the trees, sat on big limbs with their fluffy tails arched up over their backs and scolded us something unmerciful. I wish I could have deciphered their language.

There wasn't any brush to cut here. To make a nice trail, we dug and scraped the dirt across a two-foot-wide space. We blazed trees as we threaded through them. Across the canyon, we could see deer feeding in small grassy openings. At last we came to the big brushy patch of downed manzanita.

"Leona, this is going to be the toughest job of all, to get through this tangle."

"Let's just clear enough to get through; then we can work on the grading part with pick and shovel."

We worked on the manzanita, Dad sawing most of it with his four-foot cross-cut saw. "You know, Leona, I think I'll cut some of this in stove lengths and pack it into the cabin on Jimmy. It would make great biscuit wood."

"Golly, it sure would."

Time went by fast, and Dad pulled his gold watch out of his pocket. "Say, Leona, it's one-thirty. We'd better knock off for today. We've made a good start."

"That time already? Let's quit."

We dropped our tools and walked back to the horses. Betty nickered at the approach of Dad. Jimmy, his solemn little self, never said a word or batted an ear. I wondered what went on in his mind.

Trail work was like everything else; no hurry or time limit. We rode out to the job each day and tied the horses. Sometimes we would put in an hour's work, other days we'd work four or five hours, all depending on what we felt like doing. I guess that is one advantage of being your own boss. Some people are blessed with the idea, "Oh, I'll start tomorrow." Well, of course, the folks that figure that way rarely get anything done.

I took plenty of time out to go riding on Jimmy and get meat to eat. I enjoyed the solitude of the great outdoors, and I really didn't miss people very much, although I always enjoyed company who took the time and effort to hike in to visit or spend a weekend with us.

When the children came, I had fun with them. Dean, of course, always wanted to go hunting. Dorie and Joyce and her sister DeeDee were smaller. Their great delight was sleeping in the living room loft. They'd always "forget" something after they climbed the ladder to get to their beds for the night, just so they had an excuse to go down the ladder and climb back up.

When Dad wanted to relax, he cut wood. Frequently, he'd sit down on the hillside and pull his saw back and forth. Part of this was due to his terrible hernia, which is why he didn't do much hunting or horseback riding. He'd sit by the hour sawing and humming the same little tune.

During that winter I ran a trap line and caught quite a few coons, skunks and foxes and occasionally a wildcat, or bobcat, as we called them. Furs, like everything else, had little cash value. I was disappointed when I received my winter's wages for trapping. It was less than ten dollars, almost unbelievable. I thought the fur buyers were taking advantage of the situation.

I was not only mad, I was sad that the poor little animals had died for such a useless cause. I never trapped another season while on the homestead.

All winter long on days between rains we worked on the trail. We dug out cedar stumps, remembering the night Walter and I had stumbled around in the dark on the other trail. We routed the trail around all the big trees. It was picturesque the way the trail wound through the park-like trees. After the trail was finished and graded by shovel and mattock, it was a fine trail to hunt from and a joy to ride or walk on. There were always deer to watch just across the small canyon. The grade followed the rise of the little stream all the way around the mountain to the pack station. Long before it reached the pack station, the stream gave out.

Once in deer season, Walter and I trudged up the stream bed. The headwaters were halfway around the mountain. Woodwardia ferns, their fronds about five feet tall, grew all around the hole that was gushing water out of the ground. Where the water flowed into the creek, the ground was thick with glossy deep green leaves of azalea bushes. All spring long, the canyon was laced with the sweet spicy aroma of the white and yellow blossoms.

Sometimes, when we were grading out the trail with mattock or pick, we'd dig up a bulb, take it home and plant it in the yard. I wouldn't know until it blossomed what it was, but I presumed it was a brown lily or mission bell. The deer liked to eat them, so I didn't find very many.

I later traveled the trail on Jimmy after a big rainstorm and watched deer grazing in the welcoming sun that reflected its warmth off every manzanita bush.

At that time of the year you couldn't tell the bucks from the does. It was one of my joys to count the deer. One time I rode around the trail and counted over 65 deer on the hillside across the canyon. In winter and early spring they fed in large herds. It was a great place to hunt from during deer season.

CHAPTER 29

JIMMY'S SURPRISES

Everything seemed to happen out on Fir Mountain. After a rainstorm that poured buckets of water, when the heavy clouds had left the country and there was a lot of blue sky for a change, I said to Dad, "I'm going to saddle Jimmy and take a ride out over the mountain. Probably be gone a couple of hours."

"All right, Leona, I'll stick around the cabin and keep the fire going."

Across the flat the rocks were still wet and glistening in the sun, and everything looked clean after the big rain. Jimmy was trying to find something to shy from, which was a habit with him. I rode up the peak of the mountain through the dripping fir trees and wondered why I didn't find some hog rooting. Happy was wondering, too. She kept looking up at me as though I could do something about it.

Out on the long grass-covered ridge that extended down to the low divide, I saw people coming. All of a sudden, Jimmy stood on his hind feet, whirled around and galloped back up the ridge about fifty yards. He whirled again facing downhill and let out two big snorts. This was the first time he'd pulled this trick, and he sure took me by surprise! His ears pointed straight forward. When I looked down the ridge, I saw four people, one of them wearing long-haired white Angora chaps. The funny part was that he was riding a little Shetland pony and his feet were almost dragging on the ground.

"Oh, Jimmy, for goodness sake, that's nothing but a Shetland pony that's even smaller than you are." I kicked Jimmy in the ribs and started down towards them. Jimmy had other ideas. He whirled again and tore up the mountain a ways, then whirled around and snorted a couple more times.

It's a good thing the opening was large, because I never got Jimmy closer than forty yards from them. They hollered to me, "We're from the Oatis Ranch, looking for a wild hog!"

I hollered back, "Go ahead, there might be some on the north side of the mountain!"

It had taken four tries to get this close, so I rode off to the south side to please Jimmy and to get past them as best I could.

Down the ridge we jumped some deer out of a thicket of live oaks. There didn't seem to be many animals out feeding, so I headed back for the cabin. I didn't hear any rifle shots. I guess the people never found any hogs. They didn't have a dog with them, and it's hard to get hogs without one. A wild hog is much wilder than a deer. Deer have more curiosity; they will go a ways and stop and look back at you. A wild hog won't stop running for a quarter of a mile at least.

Jimmy never got over his new stunt. Sometimes we'd come upon a cow lying under a bush. In a split second, Jimmy would turn around and run the other way as fast as he could. Then he'd stop, whirl around and snort.

I think it was a carry-over from his grammar school days. One of Elmer Brown's neighbor girls used Jimmy for several years to ride to school, and some boys probably hid behind the brush and, for a prank, jumped out when she rode by. That's just a guess; I really don't know.

One blustery day in March, Dad and I rode up to the pack station. Dad was worried about some rolled barley we had sacked up there and covered with painted canvas. He was afraid it had come uncovered in the heavy wind, but everything was fine.

"Let's ride up to the Smith orchard," I said. "We might find a hog. We really need some meat."

When we got up on top of the ridge the wind was blowing a gale, and it was cold. We didn't even see a jackrabbit. I guess the animals had better sense than we did.

"Let's get out of here!" I said. "I should have known better. I'm going to get off and walk down the grade and see if I can't get warm."

I pulled Jimmy's bridle reins over his ears so I could lead him, and Dad did the same with Betty. We'd hiked about half way down the ridge when I saw Frank Fry right below us, climbing up the bank to get to the road. I turned to tell Dad about the time Jimmy nearly jerked me off my feet when Jimmy let out a big snort and, boy! he was on his way. He ran by me as I tried to stop him with the reins. I just had time to notice that Frank had on a great big sheepskin coat with the collar turned up and a big hat on his head. He was trying to pull himself up the steep bank on hands and knees.

I was almost flying, holding on and taking steps about six feet long. Jimmy was really scared. His neck stretched straight out and he was pulling me like I was a feather. I finally had to let go of the reins. Maybe Jimmy thought Frank Fry was a grizzly bear, or the devil, or something terrible.

I had visions of Jimmy running until he dropped; I'd never catch him. Mrs. Brown had told me, "Never turn him loose, you'll never catch him." Sure enough, Jimmy was clear out of sight. I walked down to the pack station and there was Jimmy standing up against the corral fence, shivering and looking back up the mountain. I started to talk to him in a low voice to quiet him. "Whoa, Jimmy. It's all right, nothing is going to get you. Whoa, stand still."

My tone, and the fact that nothing else was near except for Happy and me, gave him confidence. He quieted down and I was able to get close enough to stroke his neck and get hold of his reins. He was shivering and quivering all over as if from a severe chill. I continued to talk to him and stroke his neck, then I led him around a little. By the time Dad got down to us, Jimmy was his calm and merry little self again, though his ears really perked up when he heard Betty and Dad coming. He immediately hee-hawed to Betty.

"Say, you were really flying there for a while," Dad said. "I was afraid Jimmy would pull you off your feet."

"I let go before that could happen, but I'm good and warm now."

"The walking warmed me, too. I can feel my blood circulating again."

"Let's get to the cabin with these animals. We should have more brains than to go up that ridge on a day like this. What did Frank Fry have to say?"

"Oh, he thought his horses had gone up the road, and he wanted to head them off, but they never showed up."

Jimmy and Betty moved fast, thinking of the barn and rolled barley. We made it home in double time. When we arrived at the cabin, Dad said, "I'll take care of Jimmy and Betty. You'd better stir up the fire."

I soon had a roaring fire burning in both stoves, and when Dad came in the cabin was already warm. He told me that Betty and Jimmy had thanked him for the hay and grain and warm little barn. "Betty did her little whinny for me and even Jimmy let out one of his brays."

"I'm so glad we built the barn and got the hay inside. It's more like living. I felt so sorry for Betty last year, standing there shivering. I wanted to bring her into the cabin with us. The canvas over her kept the rain off, but it was no protection against the cold. When I think about it now, I don't see why we didn't throw a blanket over her and tie it on."

"Well, we have things a whole lot better this winter than we had last winter."

"We had so little time last fall. We were lucky to get one room up before the rain. Now we have a car at the end of the road."

"Everything is well covered at the pack station, so if the clouds decide to pour water, let 'em."

"Say, we should have packed in a sack of barley. Do you have much left?"

"There's plenty for a week or ten days," Dad said. "Jimmy eats very little."

"Did I just say we have a car at the end of the road? Well, I was wrong. My car is down at Edgar Waltenspiel's place. I'd better go down tomorrow if it isn't raining."

Two weeks ago, when I'd last driven to town and back, a big rain storm had washed out a bridge just below Skaggs Springs. Some county men said it would be at least a week before they could get the road open.

"Oh my," I said, "I can't wait that long."

About that time Ed Waltenspiel drove up on the other side on his way to town and said to the county crew, "Hey! what have we here?"

"Well, Ed, it looks like you're going to have to stay home for a while."

"Ed," I hollered across to him, "we can solve this problem! You climb down the ravine and take my car, and I'll do the same and take your pickup."

The crew laughed and one of the men said, "Well, that's one way to do it, all right." Ed made a couple of trips across the ravine with my grocery bags.

"Is there a message you want to send to Evelyn, Ed?"

"Yes, tell her to get in her car and meet me here at four-thirty tonight."

And so Ed and I exchanged cars: I took his pick-up and he took my car. I stopped to inform his wife, Evelyn. "Oh my goodness," she said, "leave it to you two. You would figure some way out of the catastrophe."

I ate lunch with Evelyn, then went on my way in Ed's pickup. I didn't get far. Right after I started up Chicken House Hill at the start of the old Sled Road at Las Lomas, there was a mud slide I couldn't drive through.

I backed down to the flat, turned around and drove back to Evelyn's. I told her the story and said, "If you drive me up to Las Lomas, then I can walk in from there."

I didn't go back for two weeks. I figured the county crew would have the road open by then. We saddled Betty and

Jimmy one morning and struck out for Waltenspiel's place to pick up my Chevy, about a two hour ride by horseback.

Evelyn invited us for lunch, and we visited for a while. Then Dad said, "I'm going to start out with the horses, Leona, you can come a little later. You'll probably catch up with me."

I figured Dad would get to the pack station about the time I'd arrive. I had no trouble getting over the mud slide, since the water had drained. The mud was now hard, and the Chevy was light, so I drove right over it and arrived at the pack station the same time as Dad.

We hung the groceries on the saddlehorn and were on our way back to the cabin. There's a solution to every problem.

Pack animals passing through The Cedars, about 1933

CHAPTER 30

THE DEER HUNT

Mr. West, who lived in Santa Rosa, was an old friend of my father's. He'd spent many days at the Las Lomas ranch hunting deer and visiting with Dad. Walter or I would take him hunting; he was a good rifle shot.

One day Walter walked in and said, "Guess who I saw the other day, Dad?"

"I wouldn't have any idea."

"Mr. West. He wanted to know all about you and Leona, how you were doing and what you were up to. We had a long visit. He'd like to come up and go deer hunting again. Those were such good old times. I told him it's a rugged trip, that he'd have to leave his car and walk almost a mile around the mountain down to the cabin on Danfield Creek. I said you might meet him with the saddle horses. Do you feel up to a trip like that? I told him I'd talk to you, then set a date. You could meet him at the end of the road."

On a Monday afternoon in August, right after the opening of deer season, Mr. West was waiting for us at the pack station. As we shook hands he said, "My, it's great to see you and Leona."

"You're sure looking fine," Dad said.

"I feel good and I'm doing well. I'll be 80 in another two months. Leona, this country life must agree with you, too."

"We're doing well, considering the Depression and all."

"Do you have a nice big buck staked out for me?"

"Not exactly, but we can probably do something about

that. Let's get your luggage, and I'll pack it on Jimmy. You ride Betty. I believe you rode her over at Las Lomas. We'll walk."

"I remember Betty—a good horse."

"You had some good hunts over at the old ranch, and I hope you're successful here."

"Oh, I'll enjoy the trip anyway. I came early. Guess I'm as bad as a kid on his first hunt—I could hardly wait for this day to come. It's such a great feeling to get out into nature. I've really missed it."

While we talked, I loaded Jimmy with Mr. West's luggage, then he shoved his rifle into the scabbard and swung up into Betty's saddle.

"Say, you did that like you've been doing it every day," Dad said.

"No, the last time I rode horseback was at the old ranch, and I guess this is the horse I rode."

We stopped along the trail and watched some deer across the canyon. I didn't spot any bucks, though. I guess that would've made a hunt too easy.

At the cabin, Mr. West got down and exclaimed, "My, what a pretty location, with the trees and the little creek and the beautiful waterfall! I enjoyed the ride, Leona, thank you."

About that time, Dean popped out of the cabin. He was staying with us for a couple of weeks to do some deer hunting. I asked, "Dean, do you remember Mr. West from over at Las Lomas?"

"Hi, Mr. West, I remember you—had the little fox terrier that rode in the grain sack tied onto the horn of the saddle. I can see him now, his head poking out the top of the bag. Do you still have him?"

"No, he went to dog heaven last year. He was getting old." Mr. West carried his things into the new bedroom.

Dad took care of Betty and Jimmy, then he and Mr. West sat out in the yard on some benches I had built under a copse of trees. I could hear them talking and visiting while I cooked dinner.

When I called them to dinner, Mr. West said, "Leona, you really have a unique cabin. I like the way you have it fixed up. This is such a fine, wild, wood-covered place with the waterfall and the little creek running down past the buildings. You built all these buildings, Leona?"

"Well, I've done a lot of the work. Walter helped Dad and me on the first room, the living room."

"I help some," said Dad, "but I'm no carpenter. I help saw logs and then pack Jimmy in with the lumber and shakes. Leona does the actual building."

After dinner, Dean helped me with the dishes and Dad and Mr. West talked politics. That didn't interest me or Dean, so I said to Dean, "Let's sit at the kitchen table and play some cards or Aggravation."

"Gee, let's play Aggravation! I like to shake the dice and see how fast I can get around the board."

"Suits me. I know I can beat you."

Dad and Mr. West talked until almost ten o'clock, then I asked if they wanted to listen to the news, and Mr. West said he did.

"You sent this radio up by Walter to Dad and me," I told Mr. West. "We've certainly enjoyed it, too. It's never given any trouble. After I got the Chevy, I bought a car battery to use on it. I exchange batteries in the car about every six weeks and run it to Santa Rosa. When I get back it's fully charged and good for another six weeks."

"Glad you've enjoyed it. I'll listen to the news, then I'm going to turn in. What time is breakfast?"

"About six. That should get us out on the mountain fairly early."

It was nice to have my own bedroom at the end of the kitchen. Dean slept on the cot I used to sleep on in the living room, and Dad had the other side. Everything was working out fine. I went to bed thinking Mr. West would probably get his buck tomorrow.

Morning came all too soon. I served hot biscuits, raspberry jam, home-made ham, fried baked potatoes and good coffee.

After breakfast, Dad and Dean saddled Betty and Jimmy. We picked up our rifles and were ready to go. "You get on Betty," Dad said to Mr. West. "Dean and Leona will take turns riding Jimmy. Hope you bring back a buck."

"We'll be back before noon, Dad."

We traveled across the rocky flat up onto Fir Mountain. We explored a small canyon on the left of the rocky flat but the only deer that ran out were does and fawns, so we moved on. I told Dean to take Mr. West out to the open country and to work around the edge of the timber. I'd wait until I thought they were in position, then walk through the firs, tan oaks and pepperwoods. Maybe I could run some deer out to them.

Even Happy couldn't find a buck for us. I walked through the timber and jumped some deer, but couldn't tell what they were.

When I arrived out in the open country, Mr. West said, "Six deer came out past me. One was a nice spike, but a spike isn't a legal buck, so I had to let him go by."

"Only two went out where I could see them, a doe and a fawn," Dean reported.

By now, it was getting pretty warm, so I suggested we go back to the cabin for lunch and try an evening hunt.

"Yes, that would be fine," Mr. West said.

I fixed sandwiches and served a jar of fruit. Dad and Mr. West visited out under the trees and really seemed to enjoy one another's company. Dad hadn't had any one to visit with for quite some time. Dean and I played cards and Aggravation, then decided it was time to go hunting, but we had no more success than in the morning.

We came back to the cabin disgusted. Maybe the moon wasn't right, or we were doing something wrong, but at the dinner table I said, "It can't be like this every day."

"Don't worry, Leona, I'm thoroughly enjoying myself."

After dinner Mr. West and Dad reminisced about their lives. It was interesting, so Dean and I listened. Dad told about working on a big grain ranch as a boy.

Mr. West said, "My father came out here in the early

1880s. I grew up in Santa Rosa, and I've spent my whole life in Santa Rosa."

We all listened to the news again, then went to bed.

I got them up earlier the next morning and, after a good breakfast, I talked it over with Dean, then said, "Let's hunt out the canyon where I killed two bucks the first day we came here."

We tied the horses in the same place, and I showed Mr. West a good stand, near where I had been on the previous hunt.

"Dean," I said, "you go around the mountain and down a ways so you can see anything that comes out the bottom. I'm going around the head of the canyon, then I'll walk down through the fir timber on the other side and into this canyon. I'll work back up on the other side, Mr. West, across from you. You'll hear me rolling rocks. It'll take about an hour and a half."

"You're the boss. I'll be right here on my stand until you come back."

It took quite some time to make my way over to the fir timber, then down almost to the bottom. I started back up and picked up a good sized rock every once in a while and heaved it down the hillside. Some of the rocks were so big, I just started them rolling and they went crashing through the brush. Some made it to the bottom. Then I heard two shots up towards the head of the canyon and thought, I guess Mr. West got his buck.

When I finally made it back to Mr. West's stand, Dean was there.

"Who shot?" I asked.

"I did," Dean said.

"*You* did? From here?"

Dean meekly said, "Yes."

"Dean, don't you realize this was Mr. West's stand?"

"I know."

"Dean, you broke one of the first rules of sportsmanship. You had no business being on this stand, and, if you were, you should have let Mr. West shoot first. It's *his* hunt, not yours."

Mr. West, good sport that he was, said, "Oh, that's all right."

I said, "No, Mr. West it *isn't* all right. Dean knows better than to take another's stand." After I cooled down a little, I asked Dean what he had shot.

"I killed a three-pointer."

Dean and I headed down to his buck. It was a big three pointer, western count. I dressed it out while Dean went back to get Jimmy. He arrived by the time I had the deer dressed out.

"Dean, grab hold of his hind legs, I'll take the forelegs and head and we'll boost him up into the saddle."

We pushed him into the saddle and I tied him down, then tied his head back over his back, so the horns couldn't poke Jimmy. Jimmy was easy to pack. He was so low, anyway, that by getting him down lower than the deer we didn't have to boost it very high. He was good about standing still.

I took Jimmy's reins and Dean and I climbed back up the hill. Mr. West had walked back to Betty. I was still mad at Dean, I wanted Mr. West to get his buck so bad. I said, "Let's take this buck and hang it, then after lunch take another hunt."

After lunch, while Mr. West and Dad retreated to the bench under the trees, I said to Dean, "If you *ever* pull another stunt like you did this morning, you can't come up here and hunt for the rest of the season. Don't you realize you have your whole life ahead of you to hunt, and Mr. West may not have many more hunts? You had no business up there on his stand. This hunt is *his*, not yours. Understand?"

"I'm really sorry I did it, Aunt Nono."

"Do you want to go out in the yard where the men are telling stories?"

"No."

"Well, let's do a little exploring. You can take your fishing rod and a fly or two, and we'll walk down through the roughs, starting at the lower end of the flat. I've never been down there."

"Can't I take a few worms?"

"You can go down to the barn and dig some."

"I'll just take my rifle."

As we walked past the men, I stopped for a minute. "Dean and I are going down the creek a little ways. We won't be long."

There were huge rough rocks to scramble over and, oh, the deep dark holes full of cold running water. Dean dropped a baited hook in one where there was a little waterfall. When the baited hook eddied in behind the falls a big fish grabbed it. Dean pulled on it so hard he broke his line.

"Oh! Nono, did you see that?"

"But why did you jerk him so hard?"

"He scared me!"

"You might as well let me put another hook on your line. Then bait it up again and go to the next hole."

Dean handled the next one better. It wasn't a very big trout, only eleven inches long. I cut a pepperwood switch to string the trout on. In a short length of rough stream, Dean caught eight nice trout. One was almost fourteen inches long.

I said, "We can have fried trout and French fries and a salad out of the garden for dinner tonight. I think we're far enough down. The creek is more level and open here, so we'll walk up to the saddle trail and back to the cabin."

Dean had to show Granddad and Mr. West the trout. "Boy, those are nice trout! Did you catch all of those, or did Leona?"

"No, Mr. West, I caught all of them. Nono says we can have them for supper."

"Are you ready to go out hunting again, Mr. West?" I asked.

"Sure, I'll go this evening. Then, tomorrow, I'll get my things together and after lunch go up to my car."

Our evening hunt was as bad as the morning hunt, and we

had no luck finding a legal buck. After breakfast next morning, I asked Mr. West if he didn't want to take a short hunt.

"No, I'll visit with your dad."

After lunch, Dad and Dean went down to the barn and saddled Betty and Jimmy and brought them up to the cabin. I packed Mr. West's things on Jimmy.

"Nono," Dean said, "I'll stay here with Granddad."

"Mr. West, do you have any cartridges in your rifle?" I asked.

"No."

"Well, better put some in the magazine. Going up the new trail we just might see something."

He picked out some cartridges and pushed them into the magazine of his Winchester, then shoved the rifle into the scabbard. He shook hands with Dad and thanked him for a good time. "I'll try to get up to see you next summer. Goodbye, Dean."

We were off to his car, and I led Jimmy. As we came to the different openings where we could see across the canyon, I looked for deer. We were halfway around the mountain when I spotted some in a small manzanita patch. We stood there a few minutes watching. I was looking through my field glasses and whispered, "Mr. West, there's a buck in that bunch. Better get your rifle out."

He got off the horse, pulled his rifle and eased a shell into the barrel. Just then, the buck stepped out into the open and I could see he had a nice set of horns. I said, "Okay, take him."

Mr. West stepped out from behind Betty, took careful aim and fired. I heard the bullet go "thunk" as it hit its mark. The buck went crashing to the bottom of the canyon. "You got him!"

I tied Jimmy to a limb and we slipped and slid down to the little creek. The buck had fallen into a pool of water. We got hold of his horns and pulled him up on the gravel bar.

"That's a nice buck, Mr. West."

"Yes, it is. It's going to be a job to get him out of here."

"I'll dress him out and we can take him by the legs and boost him up the hill a step at a time. It's not very far."

We soon made it back up to the trail, loaded him onto Betty and continued on our way.

After we'd loaded everything into his car, Mr. West looked at me, grinned, and said, "Leona, you have really made my day. I've enjoyed myself so much, it was just like the old time hunts. Don't be too hard on Dean."

"Well, he's got to learn a few things about hunting. That it's not all his way."

"God willing, I'll be back next year for another visit with your Dad, and some more good hunts."

We shook hands and I watched as he drove off up the mountain. The next spring we were sorry to hear that Mr. West had passed on to other hunting grounds. I was thankful he'd had that last hunt.

Mr. West and Walter's son, Dean, in 1934

CHAPTER 31

CLOWNS OF THE WOODS

Every night a wood rat invaded the kitchen. Wood rats always bring something to replace whatever they take. When they took my walnuts, they brought me seed balls from little cedar trees and left them in the middle of the floor. I didn't mind that, and wood rats are clean, but they made so much noise with the walnuts that they sounded like a team of bowlers in a raucous bowling alley before they packed them off. They also dropped silverware, took pot holders and just about anything they could move. One was scampering on the shelves and skating on the dishes, so I thought I should do something about it.

I loaded an old air gun with bb shot and stood guard the next night. I was ready for him. I left the kerosene lamp turned down low. About eleven o'clock, I heard Mr. Rat out in the dishes. I tiptoed out, lamp in one hand and air gun in the other. Sure enough, there was a big rat on the dish shelf hidden behind the sugar bowl. I held the gun out at arm's length and slowly poked the sugar bowl away, then shot him in the head, which put a stop to his dirty work.

In early fall, Dad and I rode over to visit with Mr. and Mrs. Chester Phelps. They owned our old ranch now, having bought it from the people we'd sold it to. Chet said, "Ann wants to visit with our daughter in Burbank, and I'd like to go, too. Would you come over and take care of things for us?"

I said sure. Dad asked, "How long do you think you'll be gone?"

"Probably two weeks. You could put your saddle stock up in the barn. There's plenty of hay, feed for your dog, and you can move into the house. We have 700 laying hens and, Leona, I take the eggs in once a week and bring back feed. I get it from Poultry Producers in Healdsburg and leave the cases of eggs there. You can use the ranch truck for that."

There were three cows to milk, two saddle horses to feed, pigs, and about 300 head of sheep out on the range.

"When do you and Ann want to leave?" Dad asked.

"It's quite a drive down there," Ann said. "Do you think next Monday would be all right?"

I replied, "That's as good a time as any for us."

"Oh! I almost forgot, Leona. I shut the hens in the big house every evening so the coons don't get them. Sometimes I have a terrible time driving them in there. I have to run them all over the orchard. Of course, I shut them up before dark, when I milk the cows. I suppose that's why I have so much trouble. Why don't you and your Dad come over Sunday afternoon and we'll leave early Monday morning? There are plenty of groceries stocked in the store room. Just make yourselves at home."

We were pretty good friends with them. I'd helped Chet and Ann and her sister catch some little wild pigs. They had them shut in a pen, now. They'd grown a lot and weighed about 150 pounds apiece.

I'll never forget Ann's sister. The day we went after pigs

she spotted them first and hollered to us, "There's the pigs, running up the hill! There goes all the profit, running away!"

Happy soon had them rounded up and we caught two of them. Ann's sister fell on one and caught it by getting her hands on its back. She shoved it hard against the earth, then sat there screaming, "What'll I do with it? What'll I do now?"

I hollered back, "Hang on! I'm coming with a sack!"

That was quite an experience for her. She'd never tackled a pig before, let alone a wild one.

Sunday evening Chet showed Dad how much grain he fed the cows, and he showed me how much mash and grain to feed the chickens. Monday morning we all had an early breakfast and Chet and Ann were on their way.

Then Dad went down to milk the cows, and walked into a problem. Chet and Ann, being city folks, made pets of all their animals, including the cows, so when Dad turned them loose from the stanchions in the milk barn and opened the door, they hurried out, stomping all over Dad's feet. He carried a couple of buckets of milk up to the house, madder than a hatter! "I'll fix those so-and-so cows! They're not going to walk all over me when I open the door! I might as well be a bullfighter, jumping out of the way to keep from being trampled. I'll fix 'em!"

After breakfast I saddled Jimmy for a ride out on the ridge where quite a lot of the sheep were grazing. There was no way of knowing if they were all there without getting them into the corral and counting them. Chet hadn't said anything about that, so I presumed they were all there.

That evening Dad was ready for the cows. When he opened the door, he was armed with a good stout picket. As they charged the door, he gave each a good rap across its nose with the picket. That stopped them and made them think. When he came in with the milk, he had a different story.

"I sure put those old heifers in their place. They respect me now."

That evening I tried Chet's method of putting the white leghorns to bed, but I didn't have any better luck than Chet. I said to Happy, "There's got to be a better way." Happy was a good sheepherder, so I thought I'd try her on hens. Next day I spent all afternoon with her, driving the hens around to get them used to Happy. It worked: Happy was very gentle and slow with them.

By the third evening all I had to say was, "Happy, it's time to put the old hens to bed." She ran out and worked them all into a flock and drove them over to the ramp and up into the house, then stood there and waited for me to shut the door. I always petted her and told her what a nice dog she was.

I gathered the eggs a couple of times a day, cleaned them with a small sandpaper block, then placed them in egg cases made of light pine wood that held fifteen dozen on a side or thirty dozen to a case. The hens were laying seven cases a week. I took them to town once a week and brought back mash and grain.

The sheep seemed to be doing fine. I rode out on the range twice a week and checked the line fence between Chet and the neighbor on the north. It was in good shape, but I found a different story when I rode the north pasture fence. It had been cut, and there were about 75 of the neighbor's sheep in Chet's pasture. They had it pretty well eaten down.

We'd had a lot of trouble with this particular neighbor when we had the ranch. One time I found eighty head of his sheep on our side when the fence was all up tight and in good shape. He had driven them around the back way and let them through the gate on the road. I was mad!

I rode back to the ranch buildings and told my brother. "We have to do something about this," I said. "There's always a big band of his sheep in our pasture."

"Well, what do you suggest? The neighbors all complain of the same thing."

"But none of them *do* anything about it, Walter. I suggest we go out there, run them into the corral at the schoolhouse tree, shear about twenty head of them and hold the wool for the pasture bill. Then we'll turn the sheep back on his side of the fence, and I'll write him that when he pays his pasture bill we'll give him his wool."

"I'm game; let's do it."

And we did. I wrote the letter, but we never heard from him or saw him. For six months, whenever we met him on the road or in town he didn't speak to us—but we never had another one of his sheep on our ranch.

Now I had run into the same thing again. I said to Dad, "They're not my sheep and this isn't my ranch, so I'm not going to say anything. I'll tell Chet about it when he gets back."

About four days later this neighbor stopped by. I guess he was surprised to see me there. "Where's Mr. Phelps?" he asked.

"They're on a trip. I'm in charge of the ranch. What can I do for you?"

He stuttered around and finally said, "I have one of Chet's bucks shut up in the Miles orchard. I thought maybe he could pick him up."

Perhaps I should explain that he was talking about a male sheep. "Is it in a corral?" I asked.

"Yeah."

"Well, that's all right. I'll drive the truck down this afternoon and get it."

I said nothing about his sheep being in the north pasture, and he went on his way. Dad accompanied me to fetch the buck. We loaded him into the truck, hauled him back to the ranch and turned him into the pasture with the rest of the bucks.

During the rest of that week, I took care of the chickens and made a trip to town. The first of the following week, I rode down along the north line of the pasture to scout the situation. The sheep were all gone out of the pasture and the fence was pulled back across the opening and wired up tight. I never heard a word about it. I met the man again about a year later in town, but not a word was said about it.

Meanwhile, two weeks had gone by. I received a letter

from Ann and Chet: "We are going to stay another two weeks, if that's all right with you," they wrote. I wrote back and said okay. Then another two weeks went by without a letter from them. Two weeks after that, they drove in late on Saturday afternoon.

I told Chet about the things that had happened. Chet and I strolled down to the orchard to watch Happy put the chickens to bed. I said, "Happy, it's time to put the old hens to bed."

As we stood there by the door, she rounded all the hens up and drove them over to the house and up the ramp into the hen house. Then she stood guard in the doorway, waiting for me to shut the door and tell her what a nice dog she was.

All Chet could say was, "If I hadn't seen that with my own eyes, I never would've believed a dog could do that, and do it so easily and without scaring the hens! How long did it take you, Leona, to teach her to herd them?"

"Just one afternoon. I sat down here with the hens all afternoon and let her work around them and be with them so they were used to her. After that, every evening was just like tonight."

Dad and I rode home the next morning. We had been gone six weeks and were anxious to get back to the cabin. When we arrived home and tied the horses, I walked over to the cabin and opened the door. I was shocked!

"There's been someone here, Dad! We've been robbed!"

Dad rushed over and looked in. "My gosh! It looks terrible. This place is a wreck!"

"Holy smoke, Dad! Even the curtains are gone."

I entered the kitchen, slowly turned around, then laughed. "Dad, I think the wood rats have moved in with all their relatives. What a mess this place is! I guess they think they have squatters' rights."

I was shocked to see such destruction, but the more I looked the more I laughed. They'd taken everything they could move and had made a big nest under my bed. When I dug it out, I found my silverware, pens, pencils, cards, small tools, and more.

The kitchen was a horrible mess. The rats had spent a lot of time going down to the barn and bringing back rolled barley with which they'd stuffed the two stoves chock full. As if that wasn't enough, they stacked a neat pile of horse manure in the center of the kitchen floor! It was dry, so I was able to sweep it out easily. Fortunately, all the groceries were in cans with lids on them. The bedding had to be washed, and it took me the rest of the day to get the cabin cleaned up so we could live in it that night.

Ah, the joys of being a homesteader.

CHAPTER 32

NATURE'S SHOWS

One evening in June I decided to take a nature walk all by myself. Happy wanted to go with me, of course, but I said, "No, you stay here and guard the cabin."

She looked at me, cocked her head on one side, looked at me again, and as much as said, "I don't believe it."

"That's right," I said, "stay here."

As I hiked down the flat and looked back, she looked so forlorn. It was seldom she was not included.

I crossed the rocky ridge where the little lizards on their rocky verandas looked over their domain. My walk around the trail and into the fir timber was nice and quiet. Not a single thing stirred. Then it changed. Gray squirrels started chattering away and chasing one another around the large trunks covered with heavy gray bark, playing tag.

The trail through large firs and pepperwoods wound its way up towards the pack station on the north side of the mountain. We'd spent many hours working on this trail, and now it was a joy to walk or ride through. I looked across the small canyon and saw several deer. If you're quiet, you can sometimes see a little fawn nursing.

While I stood there, I noticed a skunk approaching me down the trail. Quietly I stepped behind the trunk of a large fir. Mother skunk had four baby skunks following in single file along the trail and, just when they were opposite me, one of the babies fell over the edge of the trail and rolled down the hill.

He must have made a little noise, for the mother skunk stopped. Evidently telling the other babies to stay put, for they never moved, she slowly made her way down the bank to rescue her baby. She picked him up by the nape of his neck and packed him up to a half-buried log. Placing him on it, she sniffed him and then turned him over and sniffed his underside. I guess she decided he was all right, for she picked him up again and carried him onto the trail behind his waiting sisters and brothers. Then she went to the head of the line and they all continued on their way again—never knowing they were putting on such a delightful little show for me. The babies had pretty white spots on their heads that broke into two white stripes that ran down their backs into a single stripe out to the end of their tails, with the rest of their bodies in black fur.

There are three kinds of skunks. One has broad white stripes, another has narrow white stripes, and the third is all black except for a white spot on its head that fades out as it runs down the back of its neck. There is also the civet cat, which is black and spotted all over with white. He too is potent, bearing the same offensive skunk scent, which he shoots in a horrible yellow spray from a sac under his tail. When you see one arch his tail over his back, look out! Skunks can spray up to thirty feet.

Happy had been watching for my return. When I reached the rocky ridge, she came bounding up the trail to greet me with a big smile. She showed me all her front teeth and, when I petted her, she was happy again.

Nature usually entertains you in a quiet way. Early one morning in late spring or early summer, I was out for a ride on Jimmy. It was quite foggy when I left the cabin. I rode out over Fir Mountain, and all the bushes and trees were dripping with moisture. I was gone for two hours, just poking around, and saw some deer and a jack rabbit or two.

The canyon of cedars beyond the cabin looked like a forest decorated with little diamonds. The sun reflected off the drops of water that clung to the needles on the trees. All of a sudden, the whole canyon turned into millions of rainbow colors, created by a slight breeze that turned the droplets of water into prisms. The breeze died down, the diamonds returned; the soft breeze blew and the hillsides turned into a rainbow of colors once more. I sat there on Jimmy, amazed at the natural show. The sun gradually evaporated the droplets of water, and the show was over. It was a fascinating sight. I had seen it before but never in such a magnificent display over such a wide area.

When I rode back to the rocky flat with the scrubby manzanita brush it was about dry. There's always something to watch, if you'll take a few minutes to relax and enjoy it. It may just be an ant hill with ants scurrying here and there, carrying seeds back to the nest. Ants are such energetic workers.

In the spring, you might be lucky enough to find a male northwestern timber grouse on the ground in mating season. He will strut just like a turkey gobbler and, when he's strutting, his wing feathers scrape the ground. The feathers on his neck turn back to reveal a perfect orange circle about the size of a twenty-dollar gold piece. Just before he does this strutting act, he perches on a limb close to the trunk of a big Douglas fir and drums. His drumming call can be heard over a long distance by any potential mate.

A full grown grouse is a little bigger than a Cornish hen. A young grouse about three or four months old tastes as good as a young frying chicken. I always tried to get some in the late spring.

Yes, there's always something to watch in nature, but you have to be quiet and relaxed. Maybe a bird will fly close to you, a couple of hummingbirds, perhaps. They have a beautiful bronze coloring around their throats. An insect might move through the grass, maybe a grasshopper. They're all interesting to watch. Hardly a day went by that I didn't see something worth watching.

CHAPTER 33

FIREWOOD

In the spring of the fourth year that we lived on the home-stead, I contacted the man who owned the 5,000-acre ranch that the old Smith orchard was on, where the grove of black oak was located back on Hazel Hill. This was the section corner where my brother and I started our survey from. I received permission from the ranch owner to cut wood in his grove of medium-sized, straight, tall black oak. It was approximately four miles from my cabin by horseback. Dad and I talked it over and he agreed to help me cut four-foot wood. Business conditions were improving and I felt there would be a good market for wood delivered to Santa Rosa in the fall and winter.

I made a deal with Walter to stack the wood at his place. He would saw the four-foot pieces into twelve-inch heater wood and deliver it for me. So on the first of April, Dad and I saddled Betty and Jimmy and tied all our tools except for the cross cut saw on the saddles. Dad carried the saw, which was six feet long and an awkward thing to carry on a horse. We wrapped it with grain sacks so it wouldn't catch on small limbs along the trail, and he carried it over his shoulder. We also brought Dad's four-foot crosscut saw.

I fixed lunch and a jug of water to take along. The ride would take at least one hour each way, so we figured on working six hours each day, which would make for an eight-hour day. The first week we worked only about four hours a day to get our muscles hardened. I thought we might make some money. I had to stay on the homestead at least another year to prove up on it and get title to the land.

We sawed four-foot lengths to haul down to Santa Rosa in the fall. The grove was on a sidehill and the road ran along below it, so when we felled a tree I first trimmed all the limbs off, so we could slide it down to the road, then Dad and I sawed it. We split each piece in four or six lengths, depending on how big it was. Then I cut a limb three inches thick and five feet long. Dad drove that in the ground eight feet out from a stump and we corded to that measurement. By the time we quit cutting wood in July we had thirty cords stacked up.

We could have used the Chevy from the pack station to reach the woodyard, but by riding the horses we could let them graze while we cut wood. That way they got their daily feed of grass.

Nearly every day there were deer to watch in the old orchard and sometimes we saw a nice big buck or two. We also spotted some big rattlesnakes around the orchard. I think they came in to the spring for water.

One summer day, I rode out over Fir Mountain and, when I came back down almost to the rocky flat, I saw a big puff or cloud in the canyon above the cabin. It looked like smoke. I stopped Jimmy and sat there a few minutes trying to figure it out. Everything was so dry, and all I could think of was that a forest fire was starting. Then another cloud rose from the trees, and it looked to me like it had a yellow cast to it. The wind was blowing in little sharp gusts and that seemed to be when the cloud would appear.

It was coming from the head of the canyon above the cabin. Now it was down closer to the cabin. It really had me worried for a while. Then I figured out what it was. It was pollen from the trees. A quick gust of wind shook the trees, which were ready to burst forth, and the trees just exploded pollen, and the breeze carried it off in the air. Never had I seen so much pollen, though I'd seen it leave a fir limb once in a while in a tiny puff of powder. It was another one of nature's shows, put on for my benefit.

Walter was using the truck in Santa Rosa. He had five acres of prunes to pick and haul. He picked some other nearby ranches, so I couldn't get the truck to haul the wood until he was through with the prunes.

I was busy, too. I stayed with Walter and Maude for a month while I worked at one of the hop ranches, running the elevator hook to take the hops off the truck. The crews cut and hauled them in to the hop-picking machine, and I lifted them to the second story of the hop-picking shed. In the shed, four high school kids took the hop racks off the elevator hook and slipped them onto the rack where they were unhooked and shoved into the hop-picking machine.

In my first year there I worked on the belt with the hops moving past. I was one of six women who picked the trash out, after the hops came off the picking machine. On the second day, the foreman came down where we were working and said, "I need someone who can handle the hop elevator to unload the trucks. Do any of you women want to try it?" I said I would. "All right. It's all yours. I'll show you how."

I got along fine with it and was now working my third season on the elevator. The job lasted only four to six weeks, but I made pretty good money for that length of time.

There were two field crews hauling hops. They'd bet on who could haul the most truckloads of hops a day. They got to hauling them faster than the hop-picking machine could pick them, so I had a full rack in front of me with a truckman below hollering up for me to pick up his hops. I yelled down to him, "I can't. The rack's full. I have no place to put them!"

He came storming up the stairs, grabbed the handle of the motor out of my hand and ran that hook up almost through the roof, then banged it down on the cement floor. It was a good thing nobody was near it; he would've killed someone with that big hook, throwing it around with the power of the electric motor. Talk about a wild man. The kids all hollered, "FIRE! FIRE! SMOKE! SMOKE!"

I yelled at him, "Get out of here! You have no business up here! I'm going to get the boss!"

I asked one of the boys to go find the boss, quick. Meantime, the wild man left. I guess he found out he couldn't run the elevator hook either.

Next day one of the men told me they had a big fight in camp that night, and the bully who'd grabbed the elevator handle got the worst of it. He was meek after that and never again looked up toward me and the elevator motor.

The job was over in five weeks, so I went home. Walter would be through with the truck in about two weeks, so I could start hauling wood. The wood had dried out a lot, and I was able to haul a cord and a quarter to a load. We rode up to the pack station, where I left Jimmy tied and drove the truck over to the woodyard. Dad rode along on Betty, then helped me load the truck. I drove to Santa Rosa and Dad rode back to pick up Jimmy's rope and lead him back to the cabin. I returned from Santa Rosa in the late afternoon and walked to the cabin.

I couldn't drive to some of the wood, so I threw it down the hill a stick at a time. If I could toss a four-foot stick so it hit at the right angle, it would end-over-end itself clear onto the road.

It took me a month-and-a-half to haul the wood to Santa Rosa and stack it in Walter's yard. He had the old tractor and big circle saw from the ranch and, during the winter, he sawed it all into twelve-inch chunk wood and sold it and delivered it for me. The tractor furnished the power to run the saw.

The Depression was fading out. Businesses were doing much better and more and more people were finding work. We, too, were doing better. We had money from the wood that Walter delivered throughout the winter. Wood was always cash on delivery. Dean was learning a good lesson. He knew if he helped his Dad with the wood after school he could come up to the cabin and stay with me and go hunting.

There is always something to be thankful for.

CHAPTER 34

CALAMITY ON FIR MOUNTAIN

Deer season was in full swing. I went to meet Walter and Dean at the little picket gate down on Cedar Creek to go hunting. Walter had taken the job of patroling the Haigh Ranch to keep out the road hunters. He needed two horses, so I'd loaned him Betty and Jimmy for six weeks.

I met Frank Fry one day up at the pack station and he asked, "Where's your saddle horse?" When I told him, he said, "Well, Leona, there's no need for you to be without a saddle horse. I have four running around loose doing nothing. You might as well use one. Why don't you come down to the barnyard and get one now?"

"I'll take you up on that deal."

He caught a bay sorrel mare and tied her up, then went into the barn and brought out a saddle and bridle. "I should warn you, Leona, she's scared to death of mountain lions. She foaled two years ago and a mountain lion got after her colt."

"There's about one chance in ten million I'll ever meet a mountain lion."

"I guess you're about right. I've never seen one in all my hunting, and I've been in this country for fifteen years and more." Frank finished saddling the mare, put the bridle on her and then handed me the reins.

"Thank you, Frank. I'll bring her back to you as soon as hunting season is over. Is she used to packing a buck?"

"Oh yes, she's broken to pack. Keep her as long as you want."

I mounted up, waved goodbye and took off for the cabin. Dad was surprised when I rode up to the cabin. "Where did you find the horse and saddle?"

"Oh, I met Frank Fry up there at the pack station and when he found out I didn't have a horse to ride, he loaned me one."

Now, Walter and Dean had been over to see us, so they knew I had a saddle horse. We set a day to meet at Cedar Creek for a deer hunt. The day came, and I went down to the barn and saddled the bay mare. I led her up to the cabin, picked up my rifle and told Dad good-bye. "Be back about five o'clock."

"Hope you come home with a nice buck," Dad said. "Take care."

The morning was crisp and cool, a great day for hunting, I thought, as I rode out across the rocky flat. When I came to Fir Mountain, I took a small trail going around the south side, where I had ridden several times on Jimmy. There was a rough little ravine to cross, but I didn't think much about it. Just before I got to the ravine, a mountain lion suddenly bounded out of a brush patch above the trail! He tore down the hillside and crossed the trail forty feet in front of me. The mare whirled and jumped over the steep bank. The last thing

I remember was pitching over her head and looking up. It looked like she was going to come down on top of me.

I came to, lying in a pile of rocks. The horse was nowhere in sight. I started to move, but I hurt all over. I crawled up to the trail on my hands and knees. By then, I was all in. I sat there and rested a while. I hated to even think of getting up, but I had no choice. Somehow, I managed to get on my feet, and I made my way around the trail to open ground on the west side of the mountain where the trail came down from the ridge. I sat down again, my back and right leg hurt terribly.

I guess I'd been unconscious much longer than I thought, because it wasn't long before Walter and Dean showed up. "What happened?" Walter asked.

"Well, a mountain lion jumped out of the brush right in front of me. My horse whirled and threw me over the bank."

"Do you think you can get on the horse and ride back to the cabin? Dean and I knew something had happened. The mare came down to the gate with the reins up to her ears. She acted scared and kept looking back up the mountain."

"Hold onto her, Walter, and I'll see if I can."

She stood all right and I made it, but it hurt. I hurt all over. I was certainly glad the ride wasn't any longer. I made it into the cabin and lay down on the cot. Walter wanted me to ride out to the car so he could drive me to a doctor. He said, "Dean can stay here with Granddad until I get back."

I couldn't bear the thought of riding a horse even that far, so I said, "No, Walter, there are no broken bones. I guess I'm just badly bruised. I'll lie around here and take it easy."

They had to get back to the ranch, but Walter said he'd be back in a few days to see how I was. Dad took the bay mare down to the barn and unsaddled her. I didn't have any broken bones, but my back was so sore I couldn't bend over. It took six weeks before I felt like doing anything.

The first time Walter came over to see how I was doing, he said, "Leona, I didn't tell you that day, but you were as white as a sheet when Dean and I rode up to you."

"I'm still terribly sore, and I turned black and blue in several places. Guess I hit some awful rocks."

Even after eight weeks, I still had a pain in my back when I leaned over in a certain way. I went to a doctor and had it X-rayed, but he didn't find anything wrong. By that time my thigh had quit hurting. "Guess I'm all right," I told Dad, "although when I lean over, my back hurts."

CHAPTER 35

DYNAMITE

My brother-in-law, Elbert White, came for a week with pick and shovel to help carve out a road from the corral down around the mountain far enough to get onto my property, roughly 1,200 feet. Winona could not come as the girls were in school. This was one of the last things we did while living on the homestead, and the most dangerous. We ran into some pretty hard rock.

In the evening we talked about the rock. Elbert said, "Leona, if you'll jump into the Chevy and drive into Cloverdale for a case of dynamite and some caps, I'll blow those rocks to bits."

Elbert had worked with dynamite. I said, "Sure, I'll do it as long as you handle the dynamite. I don't know anything about it, and I don't want to learn."

Dad said, "Elbert and I will work on the road a little farther while you're gone. Maybe we can get out of the rock."

"All right. Your lunch is on the bank in the shade. I should be back in four hours. Don't wait for me to eat your lunch."

I climbed in the Chevy and stepped on the starter. The motor took right off and, after warming up, it settled into its usual soft purring sound. Such a good little car.

It was early in the morning and nature was busy everywhere. As I drove by the old orchard, jack rabbits went bouncing away. Then they stopped, sat up straight and looked around before taking long leaps out of sight. About ten deer ran out of the orchard and over the hill, probably headed for some brush patch to hide in. A little farther on, I flushed out a covey of valley quail.

I was soon out on the county road at Las Lomas. From there it was good road all the way into Cloverdale. I pulled up in front of the hardware store. When I asked for a case of dynamite, the clerk looked at me like I was out of my head. He didn't say anything. Finally, I said, "Do you have it?"

"No," he said, "but you can get it at the Asti store, down the highway towards Healdsburg about three miles."

I thanked him, climbed into the Chevy and headed south to Asti where the big Asti Colony Winery was. They had a great selection of tools at the store, as well as groceries. I bought a few groceries and asked, "Do you have dynamite and caps, and can I buy some?"

"Sure, we'll sell you all you want," the clerk said.

"I only need one case of dynamite and the caps to go with it."

The clerk loaded it all into the Chevy and said, "Be very careful with the caps—don't jar them or drop them."

"To tell you the truth, I'm not too fond of this trip. I'll be glad when I get this back to the job. My brother-in-law is going to use it and he knows how."

I headed back to Dutcher Creek Road and cut through the canyon to the Stewarts Point-Skaggs Springs Road. It was a nice ride back to Las Lomas, but then the going got much slower. I had no trouble descending the steep grade to the pack station. Now I reached the new piece of road. It was level and not too steep, but all of sudden I held a steering wheel loose in my hands. The road went one way and the little Chevy went the other way—over the bank! I stomped on the foot brake and the clutch pedal and came to a stop. I turned off the motor and pulled on the emergency brake and put it in reverse. I was on a sidehill slope. Gingerly I climbed out of the Chevy, reached back in and picked up the dynamite caps. Then I climbed the bank and set the box on the road.

I let out a big breath, then took in a bigger one. I walked

back over to the edge, looked down at the little Chevy and said, "What in tarnation happened to you, all of a sudden?"

I slid down to the car and looked under the front end and the trouble wasn't big, but oh my! it could have been disastrous. The small spring that held the tie rod to the two front wheels had broken and that let the tie rod drop down out of its socket to the ground. There was no way I could control the steering.

My stars and little fishes! If this had happened when I was coming down the steep grade I'd be going yet, and no one would have ever found anything but small pieces. Cold shivers ran up and down my back. You see, there's always something to be thankful for.

Elbert was successful with the dynamite. He blew that rocky ledge to bits. We didn't have any more rock to contend with until we came to the little rocky ridge in front of the cabin.

Elbert's car was down in Dry Creek Valley with Winona. He had ridden up with me in the little Chevy the first of the week, so there we were with no way to get to town. I didn't worry much about it, though, as Wayne Rulofson was coming out Saturday morning to look over the trail Dad and I had made around the mountain and to give us an estimate on constructing it into a road. When I got the car fixed, I think it cost 35 cents for a new two-inch long spring to put the rod back in place.

CHAPTER 36

THE ROAD

The trail Dad and I had dug around the north side of the mountain was wonderfully graded all the way, and the new section of road was a big help. All we'd talked about since finishing the trail was getting someone with a dozer to complete the road as far as the rocky ridge.

We'd made out all right selling firewood; my hop job yielded a good return; selling wild hog meat boosted our economy; and Dad's vegetable garden cut our grocery bill way down. We had some money now, so I went to Healdsburg and, after inquiring around, called a Mr. Rulofson who'd been recommended to me.

I told him I was in Healdsburg and would like to talk to him if he was interested in building about one mile of road. He said, "I live right here in Healdsburg on Matheson Street. Why don't you come up to the house?"

Matheson Street was only four blocks away, so I drove there and rang the doorbell. Mr. Rulofson asked me in and introduced me to his wife. We talked about the road, and he suggested he drive out the following Saturday to look it over. I wrote out directions and handed them to him. I said good-bye to Mrs. Rulofson and told Wayne Rulofson I'd see him Saturday morning at the end of the road.

It was a nice fall day, the first part of October 1934. Elbert, Dad and I had finished blasting out the rock and Elbert was still wondering how he was going to get home, because the Chevy was over the bank. I told him that Wayne Rulofson was coming out, so early Saturday morning the three of us went up to the end of the road to meet him. Mr. Rulofson arrived right on time. I introduced him to Elbert and Dad. "Good morning," he said. "Isn't it a great fall day?"

"Yes, and there's been a nice rain to settle the dust. Let's walk the trail so you can get an idea of what it will take to make a road in to the cabin. Would you like to join us, Elbert?"

"Sure."

Dad said he'd wait there. We started out and soon came to the Chevy over the bank. Mr. Rulofson asked, "What goes on here?" After I told him what had happened, he said he'd look at it on the way back. We followed the trail out to the flat ridge.

I said, "It's only a little further to the rocky ridge by the cabin, so let's go there."

When we came to the ridge, he looked it over and said, "It's a shame that rock is there. I could put the road right to your cabin. Let's go back to the flat and I'll do some figuring."

We walked back and he sat down, pulled a pad and pencil out of his pocket and worked some math. "I figure it'll take sixteen hours to here. If I have some time left on that, I'll shove the road around to the rocky ridge. I'll do it for $350. To get across the rock on the ridge would probably double the price."

I didn't see how he could do it for that amount of money, but that was his business, not mine. I said, "That sounds reasonable; when can you start?"

"I can haul the dozer in tomorrow, and start Monday morning, if that's all right with you."

"Sure, that's fine."

We walked back to the Chevy. He climbed down the bank and looked at the steering rod, then climbed back to the road and said, "No problem. I'll pick up a new spring and bring it out with me tomorrow and put it in for you."

Elbert asked him if he could catch a ride down to Dry

Creek with him. "Glad to have you." We all shook hands and he and Elbert left for town.

Dad and I swung up on our horses and headed for the cabin. Dad said, "I don't see how he can build the road for that price."

"I guess he needs the work. He's just starting out and probably wants to get some work done so he has some references."

Monday morning, Dad and I arrived at the end of the road, and at eight o'clock we heard Mr. Rulofson's truck coming down the grade. Dad said, "You're right on time."

"I want to see how this little dozer is going to do on this job. I'll warm 'er up and we'll be on our way."

The dozer was an Allis-Chalmers and had a six-and-a-half foot blade. I wondered aloud, "Gee, it's kind of small. Can it do the work?"

Wayne Rulofson started out by widening the road we'd dug. When he came to the Chevy, he stopped and put the spring back in the tie rod, then hooked onto the car. I got in and he pulled us back up on the road. Then he proceeded on down the road and soon reached the new trail. He was doing fine until he hit the slide where there was a lot of loose fine shale rock.

He had a hard time keeping the dozer from slipping down the hill. When he tried to climb back the shale and dozer just slid farther down. He fastened a long chain to a tree above the dozer, then took it over the dozer to its lower side, being fearful the dozer would tip over. He dug a trench with a mattock under the upper track back up to road level so he could run the dozer up to the road bed.

I don't know how many times he had to do this before he was able to cross the shale slide. From there on it was easy. He made a good grade into and out of several small ravines by dozing around the hill into the head of the ravine, then going out the other side on the same level. He wound expertly around some big fir and pepperwood trees. He was a good operator.

In three days he reached the top of the level ridge with thirty minutes left on his estimated time, so he cut the road around the hill to the little rocky ridge. He also bulldozed a good wide turn-around for the Chevy. I said, "You'd better come down to the cabin for some coffee and cookies, and I'll give you a check for your work."

Dad tied Betty to a tree, and I tied Jimmy and went in and stirred up the fire and made a pot of coffee. When Mr. Rulofson came in, he said, "My, you have a nice cabin here."

Dad said, "Yes, Leona and I have been comfortable here. I guess a lot of people have had a hard time getting through the Depression."

"Well, I for one haven't had a real easy time of it."

As we sat around the table drinking coffee and eating cookies, Mr. Rulofson said, "It's too bad that rocky ridge is there. It's solid rock, too, else I could have brought a road right up to your front door."

"Oh well, at least I'm within hollering distance, which is a long ways from what it was," I said. "I'm thankful for the road to the rocky ridge."

"Well I'd better be on my way to the pickup. I'll leave the dozer at the corral and pick it up this coming Sunday. It was a pleasure to meet you folks, and good luck with your road." He shook hands with us, turned and walked out the door. We watched him go over the rocky ridge, then heard the little dozer go chugging off around the mountain.

Now Dad and I were an hour closer to civilization. It was hard to believe it could happen so fast. During a period of four years, now going into the fifth year, I had made a comfortable home and weathered the great Depression and crash of '29. House, barn and woodshed had cost less than $5 out-of-pocket expense. I had a whale of a time doing it, too. Dad apparently enjoyed it, for he never complained and never seemed to care about going to town.

Chapter 37

The Final Papers

In the spring of 1936 I raised 1,000 turkeys in 50-50 partnership with Chet and Ann Phelps over at the Las Lomas Ranch. I made out real well in this venture. When the turkeys were sold in the fall, everything was paid for, so our profits were good.

In August, Elbert, Winona and their three daughters rented a house in upper Dry Creek so the two oldest girls could go to the Geyserville grammar school. Elbert and Walter had worked all summer with a survey gang on the ranch adjoining Las Lomas. Now that the job was over, Elbert wanted to get back in the sheep business. So did I.

The Caughey Ranch which joined Frank Fry's homestead on the east came up for rent, and Winona, Elbert and I rented it. It consisted of 1,800 acres and was a good sheep ranch. It had a good house, with livingroom, large kitchen, two bedrooms, a full bath with running hot and cold water, and a screened in porch all the way around the house as protection to keep rattlesnakes out. There were many rattlesnakes in the neighborhood, and the house also badly needed a new shake roof.

Elbert drove to Cloverdale and talked to Mrs. Rose McPherson, who owned the property, about buying new shakes. We would do the work of reroofing for her, donating our labor. She said she couldn't afford the shakes, and this later proved disastrous.

The ranch was isolated, seven miles off the county road, which meant there were seven miles of private road to keep up. It was terrible in the wintertime because the road forded the Warm Springs Creek seven times and there were no bridges, so the crossings frequently washed out.

Elbert drove back and forth from his Dry Creek home. We bought sheep and had them trucked to E. Waltenspiel's ranch, eight miles down the road. We penned them there overnight, then Elbert and I with our two dogs, Ring and Happy, drove them up to the corrals on the Caughey Ranch. We wool branded them and turned them out on the range.

The winter of 1936-37 was a wet one. During the heavy rainstorms, we lost a great many big lambs. They were practically drowned while standing up. On Memorial weekend, May 30, 1937, Elbert and I had the sheep in the corrals at the barn. Elbert was shearing them, the dogs and I were keeping the pens filled, Winona was handling the cutting gate to separate the lambs from the ewes and, in between times, I tied fleeces. Dad tossed the tied fleeces into a big bin for us to sack later.

In the house the three girls were doing the breakfast dishes. Betty was nine years old, Marylou seven, and Ann not quite three years. They came running down from the house and burst into the shearing shed. Betty said, "There's a funny noise in the house; it sounds like it's coming from the attic."

Marylou said, "It sounds like something is falling onto the ceiling."

I dashed outside and looked up at the house. Then I screamed! "The house is on fire!"

Elbert let his sheep go stringing wool all over the pen as we ran up to the house and into the porch to the front door. Elbert jerked the door open, and a blast of hot air and flames hit him in the face. I guess lanolin does not burn, for his shearing overalls were soaked in lanolin grease from the wool, but the flames only singed his hair and burned off his eyebrows.

I was trying to turn the water on at a faucet attached to a hose, when Elbert yelled, "Leona come on, we've got to get out of here! It's too hot!"

We dashed off the porch and down the driveway. The rest of the folks had come up from the barn and were standing down the driveway watching the fire. The girls were crying.

Bang! Bang! Bang! The ammunition in Elbert's Savage 32-40 rifle was exploding. My rifle, a Winchester 25-35, was exploding along with boxes of ammunition. Windows were popping and blowing out. Sheets of flame were billowing out and licking up the walls. The house was a roaring inferno! We had to back down the driveway to get farther away.

It took less than thirty minutes for the fire to consume the whole house and reduce it to a pile of hot coals and ashes, leaving only foundation timbers smoking and burning.

All the Homestead papers I had filled out to take to town to have notarized were now just a bunch of ashes. I had a list of expenses on the homestead: $25.00 for filing fee; $5.00 expense on house, barn and shed; $350.00 for the road plus $22.50 for a case of dynamite and caps; a check for $25.00 for the closing fee; for a total of $427.50 out-of-pocket expense for almost five years of homesteading. This, of course, did not cover our groceries. The sale of the pork paid for all of them.

Elbert and I had practically begged Mrs. McPherson to put a new roof on the house. We were so stunned by the sudden loss we just stood there. Ann was still crying. I found out she was crying over her new shoes. I said, "Ann, you haven't lost your shoes; you have them on."

"No, Aunt Nono, they're so slippery I can't stand up in them."

"Oh, I see. That's because they have leather soles and no heels. Come on, get in the little Chevy with me and you'll be all right."

"We have nothing left," Elbert said in a choked voice. "I'll go down and turn the sheep out on the range. There's no fenced-in pasture for them. We'll have to get in our cars and drive down to my house. Take the dogs. There isn't even any feed left for them."

Dad and Happy rode with me in the Chevy. Elbert, his family and Ring traveled in his 1935 Ford sedan. Still stunned, we arrived at Elbert's home, and he changed his clothes. I got a coat, and Dad put on one of Elbert's sweaters, then we drove down to Walter and Maude's. Winona, Elbert and the girls drove on down, too.

Walter and Maude were overcome by news of the fire. We all drove to town and bought a few clothes to get by with. When my oldest brother, Harold, and his wife heard of the fire, they gave us some bedding, silverware and dishes. Fern gave us a lot of groceries. Walter and Maude provided more bedding, plus pots, pans, cooking ware, dishes, towels, and much more. We stayed with Walter and Maude that night while Elbert and his family went back to their house.

Next morning Dad and I drove up to Elbert's to pick up some things and Elbert came with us up to the ranch. I had 125 white leghorn pullets in the shed. Elbert and I moved them into the hay part of the barn. There was an old cook stove stored in the barn, so we set it up in the shed and boiled some water. Then Elbert and I scrubbed that shed till the walls shined. Elbert drove back to his place that evening.

Elbert came back the next day with some cots. I put one at one end of the kitchen for my bed. Dad and Elbert put theirs up outside. Mrs. McPherson agreed to send up enough lumber for a good-sized two-room cabin if Elbert and I would build it. Once again, I found myself building a cabin. First we rounded up the sheep and finished shearing them. Then we sacked the wool and hauled it to town to sell.

I went to town and had new Homestead papers filled out and notarized, sent them off, then headed back. Elbert and I built a cabin and joined it to the kitchen cabin with a "Dog trot porch."

By this time, we'd rounded up the sheep and sold the lambs, making a small profit. My laying hens were doing fine.

I was taking three cases or more to town every two weeks. It was more than paying our grocery bill, which was a big help.

We made it through the winter of 1937, but soon after the shearing my right leg began to pain me. By the middle of June, I knew I had to go to a doctor. I drove to Santa Rosa and called on one of the best in town, Dr. Thurlow. He X-rayed my thigh but couldn't find anything, so he sent me to U.C. Hospital in San Francisco.

I now owned a 1932 Chevrolet coupe, which the chickens were paying for. That would get me to San Francisco in style. Fern drove me down, and we spent the day. Because I was getting around on crutches, they wouldn't keep me in the hospital overnight, so we drove back to Santa Rosa, then back down to the hospital the next day. They took more X-rays, still couldn't find anything and sent me back to Santa Rosa.

I knew an osteopath who had saved Dad's life in 1915, so the next day I went to him. Dad had been suffering from Bright's disease and was in bed in Las Lomas when Dr. F.E. Sohler told Mother he had three months at most to live. Well, Dr. Wyland, the osteopath, came up to Las Lomas to go deer hunting in August, and he told Mother that a patent medicine, Fulton's Compound No. 1 or No. 2, would cure Dad. "If you want to try it, I'll send two bottles to you when I go home."

"I'll try anything," Mother said.

Dad took the medicine and started to get better. The fluid build- up was leaving his body. He took seven bottles and was cured. He was up and working again.

Once again, Dr. Wyland came to my rescue. He X-rayed my thigh, studied the X-ray and showed it to me. He said, "You have a crack about seven inches long in your thigh bone. I want you to take this X-ray back down to U.C. Hospital. Show it to them tomorrow."

Fern drove me down again. When the crack was pointed out to the doctors, they studied it and suggested something that about floored me. They told me I had a tumor and that the only way to save my life was to have my right leg amputated. I said, "No, you're all wrong. I won't accept that as an answer."

"The only alternate treatment is massive X-ray treatments," they said, "and we're not sure it will do the job."

"I'll accept that over amputation."

"The best X-ray technician in California is Doctor Katherine Quinlan in Santa Rosa," the doctors said. "We'll send your X-rays up with you and you can report to her tomorrow morning. She's in the General Hospital in Santa Rosa."

Fern drove me over to the General Hospital the next morning and we met Dr. Quinlan. She read my X-rays and immediately set me up for a twenty-minute treatment. She told me to come back every morning at eleven o'clock for thirty days for a twenty-minute treatment. Then I was to rest for thirty days and take thirty more twenty-minute treatments. "Your leg muscles will become very sore," she said.

Elbert and I sold our lease and sheep to Walter and a friend of his, Admiral Hastings. Dad stayed on up at the Caughey Ranch. Elbert and his family rented a 70-acre ranch outside Hessle, southwest of Sebastopol, and went into the broiler business. I moved out to the ranch with them. The girls went to the Canfield School.

Thanksgiving morning I called Winona into my bedroom. I said, "My leg is wet."

When I stood up, my goodness! A cup or more of pus ran out my leg along with a piece of bone about three-quarters of an inch long. I took the piece of bone in to Doctor Quinlan the next day. They sent it to the lab where it was examined. According to the report, there was nothing wrong with it; it was just a dead piece of bone. I immediately felt better. I had lost a lot of weight, from 146 pounds down to 113 pounds.

Although I'd previously never missed a day of getting up and dressing, over the next three years thirteen pieces of dead bone worked their way out of my leg, emerging from both sides of my thigh. Needless to say, when they were moving I was not—I was flat on my back in bed. One piece was two-and-three-quarters inches long and three-quarters of an inch wide, but they were all very thin. I was left with a limp and a stiff knee.

In the meantime, Dad had come down to live with me in a small cottage on Elbert's ranch. I hadn't heard anything from my Homestead papers, and well over a year-and-a-half had gone by. I wrote a letter to Congressman Clarence F. Lee from Santa Rosa. He answered me, saying he would hunt them up.

The broiler business had hit bottom, so Elbert took a foreman's job on a stock ranch. I read an ad in the Sebastopol paper seeking a person to work in a small animal hospital. A small salary and an apartment went with the job. I said to my Dad, "I'm going in and apply for the job." I didn't tell Winona or Elbert.

I had just gotten off my crutches. The next morning, I drove into Sebastopol and limped into the small waiting room. There was a tall oil heater in the corner of the room and a tall young man stood there getting warm. I introduced myself as Miss Leona Dixon and he introduced himself as Doctor L.R. Libby, D.V.M. "I've come to apply for the job you've advertised in the paper," I said.

"I'm just starting this small animal hospital," Doctor Libby replied. "I also make outside calls on large animals. I have thirty fenced acres here on the edge of the Santa Rosa Lagoon. There's a large barn for big animals and we'll be moving into the new house on the hill the last of this month. I had it in mind to hire a young man as there's not going to be much office work for awhile, so I figured whoever worked in the office could do outside work as well, maybe fix fences or build."

I said, "I can repair or build wire fence, board fence or picket fence. I've built miles of fence."

"At times there are a lot of board dogs here and different animals to treat."

"That's all right. I've had lots of stock dogs and pets."

"At times I have horses here to be treated for bad barbed wire cuts."

202 Leona Dixon Cox

"I've helped treat lots of barbed wire cuts on dogs, cattle and horses."

"There might be two truckloads of pigs at a time to catch and hold for vaccination."

"No problem. I've probably caught more wild pigs than you've ever seen."

"Well, all right. I'll speak to my wife at noon and hold the job open for you until three P.M."

"How about wages?"

"I'm not paying much, $30 a month to start. You'll have an apartment with two rooms, bath and back porch. The electricity, water and gas heat are furnished."

"My father lives with me. Is it all right for him to come in with me? He'd like to have space for a big vegetable garden. He'd grow enough for your family, too."

"Sounds good. There's a fenced quarter-acre alongside the apartment that would make a good garden. I don't have time to do it."

"I'll tell you before I start that I've been on crutches for three years and just recently got off them, so I'd appreciate time to rest during the day."

"I think you'll have plenty of time to rest. I'm not that busy. Can you move in here by the first of June?"

"Sure. I'll go home now and tell my folks. I'll be back before three P.M. to sign up for the place."

I drove back home feeling pretty good. Of course it wasn't much money, but at least Dad and I had a place to live.

Winona, Elbert and Dad thought it was great that I got the job, and so on June 1, 1940, we settled into the little apartment. Doctor Libby, his wife, Jewel, and their three-year-old daughter Sandra were in the process of moving into their new house on the hill overlooking the lagoon.

One evening, Dad and I were sitting out on the back porch watching the moon's reflection shimmering on the waters of the Santa Rosa Lagoon and listening to the deep, harmonic voices of big bullfrogs. Little green earth frogs were thick on the screen door. I said, "Dad, I just received my long lost

Homestead papers. I worked and struggled hard for these papers, and I couldn't have done it without your help."

Clarence F. Lee had enclosed a letter that said, "I found your papers made out and in an envelope, but they had never been mailed. They were stashed away in a cubbyhole in one of the desks. Enclosed you will find your deed to the land." The papers consisted of a patent or deed signed by the President of the United States, Franklin Delano Roosevelt.

"Dad, I'm now the proud legal owner of 640 acres of soil of the United States of America."

CHAPTER 38

MORE ADVENTURES

Dogs and cats were sick or hurt when they arrived at the veterinary hospital and they left well, so I enjoyed the work very much. My leg got stronger all the time and less painful from the X-ray treatments, though my knee remained stiff. Doctors warned me I would someday fall and break my knee.

Sebastopol was a nice small town. Dad and I enjoyed his big vegetable garden, and so did the Libby family. The veterinary business grew by leaps and bounds, so I was always very busy. World War II raged on and Dr. Libby, who was in the reserves, was called up in the summer of 1942.

The Libbys closed their house and moved to Tacoma, Washington, leasing the business to Dr. Burdo, D.V.M. I continued working for him, but it didn't last: I couldn't stand his rough treatment of the animals.

Friends in Santa Rosa who came to visit told me of a job on a 2,200-acre mountain ranch on Sulphur Creek, ten miles out of Cloverdale. I contacted the owner, Dr. Crawford, a dentist in Santa Rosa, and Dad and I drove up to look over the ranch. I took the job.

A good house and a big barn stood on the place, and a huge garden spot was ready for Dad. I soon had 110 head of cattle to look after on the range, and almost 800 laying hens. I was back in the saddle! I raised some good stock dogs to help me. Horseback riding reduced the pain from my leg adhesions and loosened up my knee joint somewhat.

Everything went fine for three years, until Dr. Crawford, my employer, died suddenly. I sold off the stock and chickens and awaited the disposition of the property. One day I took a woman named Alice Burgett out on horseback to look over the place. She bought it, and I worked for her for two years. She stocked the ranch with sheep.

During this period I saved enough money to buy a seventy-acre place out of Bloomfield, seven miles southwest of Sebastopol. The ranch had about fifteen acres of apple trees on it, including Gravensteins, and a hundred head of sheep. The area was famous for its Gravenstein apples and its boysenberries. I planted three acres of berries and went on working for Alice.

The only building on my orchard was a small cabin. My father wanted to live there, so I fixed it up and he moved in. He was getting frail. I went back and forth on weekends to look after him.

In the fall of 1947, the old fifteen-acre orchard produced a huge crop of apples. Dryer apples were worth fifty dollars a ton picked up off the ground. I told Alice I had to quit to harvest them. She didn't want me to go, and asked how I was going to haul them to the dryer. I told her I'd have to buy a truck. She told me to take the ranch truck, so I hired three apple pickers and hauled apples for three months. One reason it took so long is that the trucks sometimes had to wait three hours in line at the dryers to be unloaded. I made enough money to pay off the ranch before the first of the year, and I bought the truck from Alice.

The last week in January of 1947, Dad took sick. I called Dr. Horace Sharrocks in Sebastopol. He came out and examined him and said he should go to the hospital. I had no phone, so Dr. Sharrocks called an ambulance, which rushed Dad to the Community Hospital in Santa Rosa.

He passed away on February 4, 1947. From the time he was thirty-five years old he'd had a large hernia low on the right abdomen, but would never enter a hospital for an operation. I think that was one of the reasons for his passing on. At the ranch, I'd watched him failing fast. He had just passed his 87th birthday on November 22, 1946.

A few weeks after he died, I was in the hospital visiting a friend when I ran into Dr. Libby, whose mother was hospitalized there and not expected to live. He had received his discharge from the service and was opening his hospital again. He asked if I'd come back to work.

"Sure, I'll come back—if I can live at my ranch and have weekends off."

He agreed reluctantly.

In my spare time I built an addition onto the cabin and eventually had a four-room house with bath, back porch and double garage. Since I did nearly all the work myself, the house and garage cost only $2,500 out of pocket. I built a barn for only $75.

I bought an additional thirty-five acres across the canyon to the north. It had an old Gravenstein orchard. Every year that dryer apples gave a good price, I harvested both orchards. Other years, I figured the apples were worth at least $10 to $15 a ton for sheep feed.

In 1952, Dr. Libby sold his property to Dr. John O'Brien. I continued working for O'Brien. He built a new cement-block hospital in the southeast end of Sebastopol on the Gravenstein Highway. Floors were cement terrazzo, very pretty and easy to keep clean and shiny, but my injured leg just couldn't stand the hard cement every day. In September of 1962, I told Dr. O'Brien I simply would have to quit.

In the meantime I had met Frank and Ornella Benson. She was from London and fell in love with the Bloomfield place. I put a big price on it, thinking to discourage her, but no, she paid cash for it. I kept my hundred head of sheep, but now I had no place to live, so I thought I'd build on the thirty-five acres across the canyon. It had a good well, but I tore down the house. It wasn't worth saving.

Mr. and Mrs. Cecil Hallinan lived beyond the old animal hospital. He wanted me to rent his 700-acre mountain ranch in Tyler Valley. I knew the place and loved it the first time I saw it, but I thought about it for a few days. My intention had been to build on my small acreage, but it wasn't big enough to carry my sheep.

Against all my relatives' advice—they said my leg wouldn't hold up, it was too much work—I told Mr. Hallinan I would rent his ranch. He was a commercial airline pilot and was assigned to Japan for a year. I signed the lease and moved my sheep and furniture up there on October 1, 1962. It turned out to be a great move, and I enjoyed an extremely happy time there.

During summer vacations, an aunt with a ranch is a great attraction for children. My sister's three girls had spent time with me on the Bloomfield place. Now they were married and had children, so they flocked to my mountain ranch.

I enjoyed them ever so much. We all did ranch chores in the mornings and went swimming in the big lake every afternoon. After swimming, they'd go hunting or trout fishing or do whatever they wanted. I taught the boys how to use chain saws safely, and how to use the bulldozer and the Ford tractor. I supervised them closely and in five years we never had to use even a band-aid.

The girls did the housework; I did the cooking and looked after my stock. I had bought more sheep and twenty head of cattle. After the first year, I bought the ranch, which had fifteen to twenty acres of clover irrigated by a sprinkler system that was fed with water from the lake. The boys and girls helped move the sprinkler system whenever it was necessary.

My neighbors were great. My nearest neighbors, about three-quarters of a mile up the road, were John and Alice Cox. We started up a little band. I had studied accordion through a correspondence course and taught one of the neighbor boys, Leland Smith, to play accordion. John Cox played a banjo-mandolin, and Nick Sylvester played saxophone. I gave Alice Cox a baritone ukulele and showed her some chords. I had drums, so Leland's mother played on them. For five years we played for dances, parades and wedding receptions all over the country. What fun those years were!

Leona Dixon Cox in 1990
—Photo by William M. Holden

CHAPTER 39

BEYOND TYLER VALLEY

A great deal of history came with the Tyler Valley ranch. Mr. Tyler had homesteaded the place in the early 1860s and later bought government land until the ranch had grown to 700 acres. The first stage road ran through it in the early days, ending in Kelseyville, Lake County. The road was built off Geyser Road at Squaw Creek in 1876 by Chinese labor hired by Mr. Tyler. It was a toll road.

It took two days to drive from Cloverdale to Kelseyville by stage or freight wagon pulled by four-horse teams, so Mr. Tyler built a hotel for the overnight stop. Hold-ups and robberies were common on this road.

William Cummings from Healdsburg was one of our famed stagecoach drivers. He lived until the age of ninety-two, and his wife is still living. Will was well-liked by everyone, young and old, and his funeral, which I attended on March 16, 1977, was one of the largest ever held in Healdsburg.

The Kelseyville-Cloverdale road was closed and abandoned when the Hopland Grade Road was built. It leaves highway 101 at Hopland and winds over the mountain to Lake County. A new road was built to the Tyler Valley Ranch and adjoining ranches. Tyler Valley and its creek nestle in high mountains surrounded by chamise- and pine-covered hills. Don Canevarri and his son, Fred, owned the ranch through the forties, then sold it to Cecil Hallinan, from whom I bought it.

This country adjoins the Geyser area, famous for steam wells that run huge generators to produce electricity. It's the largest geothermal steam-generating plant in the world and is adjacent to Lake County's Cobb Mountain geothermal area. Until 1890, the steam and hot mineral waters were used for medicinal purposes. A hotel, reached first by stage coach, then by automobile, stood at The Geysers for years.

After I bought the ranch, I also bought some adjoining property, so I now owned 995 acres of land—more than one-and-a-half square miles.

On the first of December 1967, I took one of John Cox's nephews, Jeff Daniels, for a wild hog hunt on Nora Henderlong's ranch. For me, it turned out to be a disaster. It was raining and slippery as we hiked over the hills, and I slipped and came down hard on my stiff knee. I heard three distinct pops, and knew I had broken my knee-joint all to pieces. I couldn't move without terrible pain, so I just lay there in the muddy blue clay and the rain.

Jeff tore off his coat and laid it over me to keep the rain off— then ran a mile back to the ranch house. Nora came up with the jeep, and fortunately, she could drive to within fifty feet of where I lay. With their help, I managed to climb into the jeep and Nora drove me to the hospital in Healdsburg.

My knee was set and pinned together and somebody drove me back to the ranch. As Jeff was now out of high school, he stayed with me and took care of the stock, did the cooking and washing, and fed my little poodle, Susie, and my stock dog, Tip, a border collie. Alice and John came over every day, too, to see how I was getting along.

In April of 1968, Jeff was hired by the forestry department out of Willits, but I could now get around on my own. Alice and John lived nearby in case I needed them. I got around on crutches and drove my pickup, but it was a year before I could do much work. I decided to sell the stock and get off the big ranch because it was too much work for me, with my leg problem. I moved a travel trailer onto thirty-five acres I bought from John and Alice, and moved in. Later I had a nice house built there. The big ranch sold immediately.

Alice and John remodeled the old schoolhouse, which was just over the hill from where I built, and they moved in.

In the fall of 1968, Alice fell sick and was diagnosed as having cancer. John and I took care of her, but in the last week of January 1970, she had to enter Healdsburg Hospital. She passed away on January 31, 1970. She and John had been married fifty years, lacking only three weeks. John was broken.

His oldest son Walter and wife Vonnie, who lived on a five-acre ranch on the Russian River a few miles out of Cloverdale, invited him to come and live with them.

Almost a year later, Walter and Vonnie sold their place and moved to Santa Rosa. John didn't want to live in Santa Rosa, so he went back to his schoolhouse on the mountain. Meanwhile, he and I had bought 640 acres that joined his mountain home. I had kept my bulldozer when I sold the Tyler Valley Ranch, and now started building eight miles of jeep road on our new property. Very heavy live oak brush covered the planned roadway. John went with me to cut brush out from the brake pedal whenever it jammed the brake rods.

On the weekend of December 31, 1971, John and I made a big decision. We eloped to Reno and got married. John liked to tell about the county clerk, a young woman who wore bangs straight across her forehead. She passed the papers to John, who recorded his age and former marriage of fifty years. She looked over my paper and noted that this was my first marriage and also that I was 69 years old. John said her eyebrows went up under her bangs and never did come down.

We decided to live in my new house on the thirty-five acres. There we played our favorite music again, and during the years to come we did quite a lot of traveling by air, ship and camper.

My old back injury from the homestead accident finally

caught up to me and put me in the hospital in 1976 for over four months. I wouldn't be here today if John hadn't been so faithful, staying fourteen to sixteen hours a day with me in the hospital.

One day a blood clot traveled from my leg to my heart and lungs. I was unconscious before I knew what was happening or could say anything to John, or ring the bell. He called the doctor and nurses, who rushed me into intensive care in seconds. The relatives were called in that night. Things didn't look so good.

I guess the good Lord didn't want me because I'm still here. I received word my twin sister, Winona, passed away on November 10, 1977. She had been widowed since Elbert died in 1972. My older brother, Harold, passed on November 16, 1980.

I was in considerable pain during the summer of 1985 when my old right leg broke in the thigh. I'd had casts, pins, rods and braces from former operations, and the whole thing finally just broke all to pieces. The decision was made to amputate. I went to the hospital on September 16, 1985, and my leg was amputated the next day.

The amputation was very high on my leg, so I've never been able to use a prosthesis. I use crutches and a wheelchair, and to get around outdoors on my little ranch at Oregon House, Yuba County, I use my all-terrain motorcycle. I still drive my van and go fishing. It may seem strange, but I've never regretted losing my leg—I got rid of so much pain at the same time.

In 1980, the doctors discovered John had leukemia and gave him only six months to live. He outfoxed them by seven years and five months. He was on chemotherapy all this time, but was up and about every day working on his electrical hobbies. He passed away April 10, 1988. We had almost seventeen years of a wonderful married life.

With John gone, I had to revamp my life style. One of the things I did was to take up writing in earnest. In 1985 I bought a computer and started to struggle with its obstinate ways. I started with poems first, then stories, and am now finishing this book. I intend to keep right on writing.

The end